"...This is a remarkable little book, meticulously detailed and yet expansive, drilling implacably toward reality yet compassionate, forgiving. Not every family buries the same secrets, but all bury truth in one way or another. *The Mike File* offers a compelling and empathetic argument for finding that truth."

—Betsy Burton, author of *The King's English: Adventures of an Independent Bookseller*

"This is a story about one family. But more, it's an American story, where mental illness hides in the shadows. I'll surely never forget the profound journey that writer Steve Trimble undertook as he faced the contents of the Mike File, the history of his brother's short life."

–Dorothee Kocks, author of *The Glass Harmonica*

"Research, imagination, and his talent as a writer of vibrant nonfiction are the tools of resurrection that Trimble uses to bring his older brother back to life in *The Mike File*. 'No one gave Mike a second thought,' Trimble writes of his brother, who has fallen through the cracks of the mental health system. *The Mike File* is Trimble's second thought. In it, he found himself, his family and the crack̲ ̲ ̲ ̲ ̲ ̲ ̲ ̲ ̲ns, and through ife of a brother

–Davi̲ ̲ ̲emains

"*The Mike File* speaks to the still silent voice that travels through all families beset with mental illness. In his pursuit to understand his brother's life and indeed his own, Trimble forces us to acknowledge the painful truths about how we treat those with mental illness. This book is a beautiful and anguished revelation."

–**Melissa Bond, author of *Blood Orange Night***

"For those of us who have long relished Trimble's words and photographs on behalf of our public lands, most recently the Red Rock Country of southern Utah, this new book focused on the private landscape of family may seem 'out of sync.' But is it? Bringing the same fierce attentiveness and advocacy to human nature, including his own, as he does to the natural world may simply be another dimension of his calling and creativity. For facing personal as well as political paradoxes has perhaps opened a path that may be leading him towards a whole new group of appreciative readers."

–**Gail Collins-Ranadive, author of *Inner Canyon:*** ***Where Deep Time Meets Sacred Space***

THE MIKE FILE

A STORY OF GRIEF AND HOPE

STEPHEN TRIMBLE

THE LITTLE BOUND BOOKS ESSAY SERIES
WWW.LITTLEBOUNDBOOKS.COM

Published in 2021 by Little Bound Books
Cover Design and Interior Design by Leslie M. Browning
Cover Images and Interior Images © Stephen Trimble
Cover Image: Mike and Stevie, Silver Falls, Oregon, about 1955.
ISBN: 978-1-953340-22-1
EBOOK: 978-1-953340-23-8
First Edition Trade Paperback

Little Bound Books is an Imprint of
HOMEBOUND PUBLICATIONS
WWW.HOMEBOUNDPUBLICATIONS.COM

HOMEBOUND PUBLICATIONS IS A REGISTERED TRADEMARK.

10 9 8 7 6 5 4 3 2 1

Little Bound Books, is committed to ecological stewardship. We greatly
value the natural environment and invest in environmental conservation.
For each book purchased in our online store we plant one tree.

In memory of my brother,

Michael Trimble (1942-1976)

and my parents,

Isabelle Trimble (1921-2002)
Donald Trimble (1916-2011)

CHAPTER ONE

All this comes from not having Good Frame
and Peace of Mind.
—Mike's letter to Isabelle, June 10, 1967

I AM SIX. I tuck between the wooden studs in the garage, folding into a ball, my hands over my ears. Buckshot sprays of angry words fly at me through the open kitchen window.

Summer heat fills the garage. I stare at the stipple of oil stains on the concrete floor and monitor the dust motes as they float from light-less corners through golden sunshafts. I jam myself deeper into the corner, aching to disappear. Anything to distract from the incoming missiles packed with anguished words.

In the kitchen of our little house in the Denver suburbs, my teenaged brother, Mike, towers over our mother, Isabelle, his arms braced around her. He cages her against the wall. Mike is big, almost six feet tall at 14. He screams at our mother.

You love Stevie more than me.

You put me in school with retards. Everyone yells at me. Everyone tells me I'm messed up. Too much trouble. Stupid. Sick.

He aims his rage especially at my father, Don, who is Mike's stepfather—for Mike is Isabelle's son from her brief-disaster-of-a-first-marriage.

I hear you and The Stepdad talking. I hear you. You want to send me away.

You hate me. I hate you.

Mom does her best to speak calmly, to talk him down.

I hide in the garage. Indeed, I hide from Mike's story for a very long time.

I can reclaim only a few moments from my earliest years with my brother. I remember Mike's silly giggle and grin before his broken brain swept him away, his in-your-face enthusiasm—a giddiness with an edge, a little too ferocious, a little unsocialized, a little manic. That daunting summer afternoon in our Denver home in 1957 eclipsed any other joyful memories.

A few days after Mike's searing confrontation with our mother, my parents, at wit's end, admitted him to Colorado Psychopathic Hospital for evaluation. Mike never spent a night at home again.

THE MIKE FILE

Years later, my brother's death made headlines. His loss wasn't just a family tragedy or even just a scandalous failure of public policy in Colorado but a national one, a replay of the consequences of the deinstitutionalization of the mentally ill.

I knew Isabelle saved the agonizing newspaper stories about Mike's death. I had read them when they were published, but for decades I felt no need to revisit them. When I finally got around to asking about the file's whereabouts, Mom told me she destroyed the packet that chronicled Mike's difficult life because she found the details so painful.

After my mother died in 2002, I mentioned to my father that I wished Mom had saved those clips. Dad told me that when he saw Mom toss the envelope, he retrieved it from the trash and hid it away. The file survived after all—a sheaf of decades-old court and medical records, yellowing newsprint, and letters from Mike. These few pages preserved the mostly-lost story of my brother's difficult life in and out of our family.

That Don salvaged and safeguarded the file shouldn't have surprised me. My father was a scientist to his core and made sense of his world by organizing facts and constructing timelines so he could analyze the incoming stream of data that composed his life. He documented his family as he documented his geologic research and fieldwork.

When I discovered that the file still existed, the focus of my emotional life lay elsewhere, with my family, with our two kids headed into adolescence. I chose to leave the file with Dad, preserved in a drawer in his bedroom.

Several years later, on a visit to Denver to see my father in his retirement-community apartment, Dad told me that he had set aside the file.

He felt it was time to pass it on, that I should take it. But when I left for home, I forgot the envelope. "Forgot."

Dad was then in his nineties, with macular degeneration taking nearly all of his sight. When I asked about the envelope on my next visit, he said, with distress, that he apparently had thrown it away as he was culling old papers. He intended to jettison something unimportant, but he misread the label and tossed the "Mike" file by mistake. Though disheartened, I knew I shared responsibility for the loss. I'd spent years evading the evidence, a lifetime avoiding the emotional challenge presented to me by my brother's life.

I skirted any thoughts of Mike's story beyond the most pat and superficial. "*I had an older brother—a half-brother—who left home when I was six. He was diagnosed sequentially as retarded, schizophrenic, and epileptic. He died years ago.*"

Then, at the beginning of 2011, we moved my father from Denver to Salt Lake City, to live in a senior-center apartment near us as he approached a frail 95. As we ticked through his inventory of belongings and sifted through his filing cabinet in preparation for the move, there it was, the envelope marked with Mom's block letters, "*MIKE*." Dad hadn't tossed it down the garbage chute at the end of the hall. The file turned out to be deathless.

Mike won't disappear from my life, no matter how "forgetful" I might be.

Dad endured the move but lived only a few more weeks. His last words to me, "I've had a wonderful life." And then, to my wife, Joanne, "Steve is a lucky man." Lucky indeed to have Joanne as my lifetime partner. Lucky to have Don as my father, Isabelle as my mother. Lucky to be free of mental illness. Lucky to not be Mike.

I left Don's papers in boxes for months, needing the time to grow comfortable with my new identity as a man bumped into the "older generation" by the deaths of my parents. When I finally unpacked Dad's archive, the clasped manila envelope surfaced again, the sole record of Mike's place in our family, along with a scattering of photos in our family albums and an artifact or two.

My brother's story has always unsettled me. I could so easily focus on the tight relationship I had with our parents after Mike left and, later, the love I share with my wife and kids. I carried fear and shame about my brother, just as nationally we carry these same feelings of disgust and discomfort about mental illness—what one psychiatrist calls "primal fear." Though I shared a bedroom with Mike for six years, I've buried nearly every memory, even the good ones. Many years ago, when Mike rejected us, when he wrote to our mother, "leave me alone forever," I felt relief.

Mike, the defining tragedy of our mother's life, has long been gone. My mother and father, Isabelle and Don, are gone. A fading circle of older family members and their inconsistent memories are all I have to successfully resurrect the details of Mike's existence. Am I too late? And where will this resurrection lead for me?

The "Mike File" feels incendiary. It's taken me a year of distance from my father's death to open it. But, finally, I unclasp the envelope and spill the contents onto my desk, each sheet of paper a clue to Mike's life. This time, I won't defer to our mother's desire to let old wounds heal and remain closed. I can no longer be complicit in erasing Mike's memory.

It's time for me to grapple with Mike's life and death and to follow the story of our mother and her lost soul of a son into the shadows of America's dreadful response to mental illness and behind the doors I've barricaded in myself.

This time, when I look into my brother's eyes, I will beat back denial and shame. I will do my best to replace complacency with compassion. I will learn to not look away.

CHAPTER TWO

Take a trip to Montana or Utopia.
I can't care less where you go or what you do.
—Mike's letter to Isabelle, July 3, 1967

WHEN I WAS ABOUT TEN, bored, I wandered out to the garage to poke around, looking for something novel, something diverting. My dad had built three shelves across the back of the garage, stacked with boxes of seldom used dishes, dusty suitcases, occasionally used tools, outgrown toys. My grandmother's wooden-shafted golf clubs from the Twenties, short enough for me to use, each iron stamped with a quaint name—mashie, niblick. My dad's well-worn custom boots, ready for the endless miles he'd walk in his next field season. I always found it eerie that a wooden model of his foot lived in the back room at White's Boots in Spokane,

Washington, poised for his order whenever he needed a new pair.

This day, I found a green metal file box I'd never noticed. The box had a locking clasp, but when I pushed down the latch, the top popped open. Inside were documents and records.

Who cared about auto titles and house insurance? But there was more, folders labeled with names: "Stevie." "Mike." Temptation overrode any concern about discretion. I pulled out the certificate that recorded my brother's birth.

The document said that "Michael David Sher" had been born on December 31, 1942, to parents identified as Isabelle Virginia Brinig, 21 years old, and... *not* Donald Trimble, but Morey Louis Sher, 30.

Line by line, these typed words burned into my brain circuitry. Our mother was married before she married my dad? The birth certificate logged a wedding in Butte, Montana—where Mom had been born into tightly connected families of immigrant Jewish retailers. I thought I knew my family. My Brinig grandparents now lived in east

Denver. We saw Mom's sister, Charlotte, and her family all the time. I thought of my mother as an unchanging, dependable constant. These were the defining walls of my world.

But who on earth was Morey Sher? How could I not know that Mike and I had different fathers? I felt betrayed.

I went to my parents' bedroom, where two framed studio portraits displayed on the dressers maintained Mike's presence in our family even in his physical absence.

One captured Mike as an alert infant in Isabelle's arms, the other as a cute pre-schooler. The photographs remained there, all through my childhood. I had never wondered why there wasn't a father in these pictures.

I could be a secretive kid. I had a rich interior life, fueled by a steady stream of books and dreams. I occasionally swiped one of my mother's Viceroys, hid in the little barn behind our house where our neighbor kept his horse, and coughed my way through a cigarette.

I knew how to keep quiet.

Isabelle and Mike, 1943.

But this time I couldn't. That "Mom" had this life before she became *my* mom, before she became "Isabelle Trimble," was too unsettling, too much to comprehend on my own.

When I gathered my courage and asked Mom about Mike's father, she wilted. She looked so, so sad. She told me that she was married briefly and moved from Montana to Denver with her new husband—who, I learned much later, had grown up here. That the man treated her badly, and that she divorced him immediately after Mike was born. I heard the same one-sentence story from her for the next forty years as she deflected questions about her first marriage. My storyteller mother—so open and voluble about nearly everything—absolutely did not want to tell stories about Mike's father.

My resentment about my mother withholding this crucial fact stayed with me. When I had my own children, I looked for an opening to tell them I'd been married before I met their mom. My two-year practice marriage in my twenties didn't matter a whit to my kids, but I wanted to make sure the news came from me. I told my daughter when she was twelve and my son soon thereafter, so he wouldn't hear the revelation from his older sister. They thought it was weird that I'd been married before, weird that I'd tell them. But I felt a powerful need for transparency. I wanted no hurtful green metal file boxes in their futures.

A HARD ROAD AHEAD

First, Morey Sher leaves when Mike is an infant—and Mike loses his dad, who makes no effort to ever again stay in contact. Isabelle and Mike move in with her parents, who have followed Morey and Isabelle to Denver from the family home in Livingston, Montana. Mom takes a full-time job, working as a clerk in the War Assets Administration. She makes her contribution to the war effort, but Mike loses round-the-clock intimacy with his mother.

Isabelle is *so* young. She is just 20 when she marries—only a couple of years out of high school. Barely 21 when she has Mike and divorces Morey.

My grandmother, Nancy, quits her new saleslady job at the high-end Denver women's clothing store, Neusteters, so she can stay home and take care of Mike. Mike has an enviable closeness to his whip-smart grandma, but this might have turned out to be more a damaging disruption than a saving grace. My older cousins have told me that Nancy might have been bipolar, that her anger could be terrifying. She could be loving, but any misbehavior from kids could trigger "hollering and screaming." I have no such memories. After several years of increasing dementia, Nancy died when I was ten.

Vulnerable Mike is now with our volatile grandmother—yet another loved one he can't depend on.

And then, here comes a stepdad.

Isabelle applies for a position as a clerk-typist with the U.S. Geological Survey in the fall of 1946. My father is one of two enthusiastic young bachelors who moved to Denver after their

service in World War II to begin their profes-
sional lives in the Survey. Dad spots Mom during
her job interview, telephones the office manager
from across the room, and says, "Quit jawing and
hire the girl!"

Isabelle gets the job. The two begin dating
soon thereafter. Don writes regularly to Isabelle
during his 1947 field season, June to October,
in blistering heat, as he maps basalt coulees and
scablands in eastern Washington State. In his
letters, tucked away by my mother, he signs off
with banter that sounds like it comes right out
of the latest Cary Grant screwball comedy, lines
that surely made Mom laugh and blush. "Hello
gorgeous," one note begins.

Dad was simply stating fact. In those days, my
mother looked dark and glamorous. She radiated
emotional intensity and vulnerability, the sensual
look of a 1940s movie-star. Hedy Lamarr, perhaps. One of my cousins affectionately summed
up Mom's pizzazz. She saw my father's extended
family "as soothing and predictable and low-key
as oatmeal. Isabelle was Lucky Charms."

Dad's relatives in his little hometown back in Washington's Yakima Valley were thick-bodied, churchgoing, conservative; grounded, warm, and generous—and a tad astonished by his choice. Dad was an only child, loved intensely. Isabelle was The Other, a slender divorced Jewish woman with a five-year-old son from her broken first marriage.

Isabelle and Don marry the day after Valentine's Day in February 1948 when Mike is five, a cute little boy. This complicates Mike's primary bond with his mother. The enthralled couple set up their new family life in an apartment, moving Mike from the only home he can remember. Two years later, I come along. More competition.

In 1951, when I'm an infant, we move again, to our own little house in the first ring of Denver suburbs, just five miles from downtown, our family home for the next fifty years. The "Trimble mansion," as our mother teasingly calls it, measures just 1,200 square feet. It takes no more than ten steps to walk from the living room couch through the tiny dining room to Mom's kitchen.

The move means that halfway through second grade Mike is the new boy in class. Mike is a sweet kid but slow to learn. I'm barely aware in these years—just four when Mike finishes sixth grade in a regular classroom after years of heroic tutoring by our mother. I have dim memories of Mom working with Mike after dinner, sitting for hours huddled at the yellow Formica of our kitchen table while Mike struggles to master basic arithmetic and read haltingly from textbooks.

Mike is labeled "mildly retarded," the acceptable term in the fifties. His report cards, saved by Mom, reflect his skills and his deficits. In Mrs. Chamblee's third grade class in 1952, Mike misses only 5 of 135 spelling words. Right through elementary school, he receives Bs in Spelling and Ds and Fs and "needs to improve" in just about everything else. The Fs are rare, thanks to our mother's hard work with him at home. Mike lasts through sixth grade in regular classrooms, surely feeling the stress of falling a little further behind each year even while proud of being a bit of a savant, remembering a long list of birthdays.

Mike (13), Stevie (5), and Don (40). Summer, 1956.

In my search for clues to Mike's life, I start with the satisfyingly familiar work of retrieving the facts. Like my geologist father with his analytic brain, writerly research comes far easier to me than digging deep in my buried emotions.

And so when it occurs to me that the Jefferson County school district might keep documents for a long time, I call to request Mike's records. Sure enough, I find notes from his teachers that track his journey year by year. In second grade: "Very weak student. Impossible to hold attention long. Picks on others, sometimes hurting them. Being passed because of size and attitude. Parents interested and very concerned."

Third grade goes no better. "A very weak student. Can take directions individually but directions given to group are lost on him. Good in spelling. Reads words but no expression in reading. Does not comprehend."

It's a litany. I can hear the teachers' concern and frustration. Their patience is eroding. Their pithy summaries of Mike's journey make me ache for my brother.

Fourth grade: "'Plays' like he doesn't know work, but really does. Social adjustment poor. Brags about self." Fifth grade: "Doesn't get along well with others. Asks for help when he doesn't really need it and doesn't listen when he is helped. Mother insisted that he can do at least average work."

Mom believed in Mike. She believed that if she dedicated enough time and energy to Mike, he could learn. Our mother had deep insecurities, but she had unflappable faith in hard work, as well.

Nonetheless, Mike's sixth grade teacher envisions a future for Mike that Isabelle's determined optimism can't forestall. "Social misfit. Not well coordinated. Has persecution complex. Michael has a hard road ahead."

SOMETHING BIG AND DARK AND ROILING

In seventh grade, when special education was new and progressive, Mike moved into the first special-ed class in our county schools. The year was 1955. Don and Isabelle were thrilled and optimistic that the pioneering program had arrived just in time to give Mike a chance to succeed. For the first time, families had an alternative to institutionalization or homeschooling.

In 1956, reporting to Don's parents on the weekly wire recording they exchanged, Isabelle described a meeting where she heard about the power of "the right type of special education." "Retarded children" in these programs could do well later in life, becoming self-supporting, owning their own homes, and even increasing in IQ. My mother was always filled with hope.

At first, the kids at Eiber School scared me with their unfamiliar behaviors, wheelchairs, and steel braces. They also were eager to play. Maybe they accepted me because I was so much younger. As a five- and six-year-old, I was safe. I soon looked forward to visiting Mike's school when our mother checked in with his teachers.

The school district archived Mike's test records. When I asked for them all these years later, I found that in seventh grade special-ed, his Bs

Eiber School class. Mike, upper right.

in Spelling became As. His Ds in everything else bumped up to Cs and Bs. Mike's IQ measured 72. At Eiber, Mike was the smartest kid in the room. Held in awe by his more disabled classmates and ignored by mainstream kids, he lived in a social no-man's-land.

And then something big happened inside Mike's brain. Something dark, angry, roiling. He withdrew from our family. In eighth grade, his final year in our county school system, Mike's marks in social development deteriorated to a sea of Xs.

One of our cousins—halfway between Mike and me in age—remembers the first few years that she knew Mike as uneventful. She "never had a sense of Mike's retardation. He just seemed like a normal everyday kind of guy. I never heard a breath about him being different than you and me in school."

I have that same sense of my brother as "normal" until that last angry year. Mike was kind to me, treating me just like a big brother treats a little squirt of a sidekick eight years younger. I loved him. But my recollections of these happier years when Mike still lived at home feel eerily fragile. I can barely pull up a few wisps for viewing, and these snippets of memory generally lack soundtracks.

Self-help writer Louise Hay believes that "we create every so-called illness in our body." It's hard to say how her New Age mantras would have worked for Mike. But when I skim Hay's list of the causes of illness, her notation for bad eyes stops me cold. My eyes crossed at two, and I've worn glasses ever since. Hay writes, "Whenever

I see small children wearing glasses, I know there is stuff going on in their household they do not wish to look at."

I've never thought of my less-than-perfect eyes as anything other than genetic bad luck. Though I've been fully aware of blocking most of my memories of my early years with Mike, it never occurred to me that I might actually have blocked my *vision*. Louise Hay takes me a step closer to acknowledging that unconscious emotions run my life, a step away from my calm, rational self-definition. Hay's insight deeply rattles me and makes my small collection of surviving memories—what I *saw*—even more precious.

I remember Mike hanging out with a neighbor boy his age. I remember Mike caring about his clothes, as teenagers do. I remember Mike playing music as we sat together on the living room floor and spun 45s on his pink-and-gray portable record player. Bill Haley & His Comets. Elvis Presley. I still have a binder of these singles—the sole physical artifact from Mike's childhood, complete with Mike's handwritten index. I also can hear Mike warning me not to mess with his record player unless I was with him. This was fine by me, as my musical taste at the time ran more toward Bozo the Clown. I was the little brother, he was the big brother. I had my plastic dinosaurs, he had his rock and roll.

I don't remember Mike playing outside. Our quarter-acre of suburbia retained a trace of Great Plains placehood, with the neighbor's horse barn behind our house and open fields beyond. An old ditchline ran across the property line, with a venerable cottonwood that turned loose on springtime winds clouds of sticky seeds trailing

Mike's index to his record collection.

their silky parachutes. Magpies flapped by, raucous and elegant. Our mom tamed a squirrel to eat from her hand and named her furry friend Perri (after seeing the Walt Disney "True Life Adventure" that brought Perri the squirrel to full, endearing, anthropomorphic life). I spent a lot of time exploring that backyard. Mike did not.

Each of our lives is a million–piece jigsaw puzzle, and the years when Mike and I lived at home together give me just the first few edge pieces of Mike's puzzle, of my puzzle.

And, then, our cousin remembers "tension." She had a gut sense that Mike had become "different."

"His looks changed," she says. "The look in his eye changed. Maybe it was just puberty. He was 13 and growing so fast he was clumsy. He couldn't make his body do what he wanted it to do. But he wasn't the same person. He was cranky. Isolated, somehow. You didn't want to cross him, you couldn't poke fun at him."

Another recitation from the Family Legend, the story we created to explain the calamity that struck our household: *Mike's frustration overwhelmed him as he entered puberty.*

He changed from being sweet and slow to cross and withdrawn. In the middle of this shift, he had two surgeries for flat feet, surgery rarely done today. Don and Isabelle had made the decision to "fix what was fixable." Immobilized for months in full-leg casts, Mike had to navigate the world on crutches and accept Dad's help in the bathtub. His dependency on his stepfather while in his casts humiliated him, and he took out his frustration on Don.

I remember Mom and Mike returning from a doctor's appointment, coming around a corner of our house, looking for me playing in the back yard. His crutches and casts unnerved me. Even though his classmates signed his casts cheerily and Mike let me add a drawing of my own, those weighty plaster encasements around his legs seemed menacing and unnatural, almost like weapons.

My fascination with my big brother faded as his moodiness escalated, as he became unpredictable. I lived on edge, anticipating an eruption of frustration directed at our mom like the afternoon his fury drove me into the garage.

Up until this time, Mike accepted Don, who had legally adopted Mike just months after marrying Mom. Don acted as Mike's father in every way. But my brother now grew bitter toward the stepfather who had arrived in his life when Mike was five, the man who had usurped the primary role Mike had with the woman both loved. Still, Don continued to give Mike all the compassion he could muster.

THE BEST CHANCE FOR HAPPINESS

Mom archived two letters from this time. One from my father to his parents. The response, from my Grandpa Trimble. Their correspondence takes me deep into the emotions in my family in this harrowing time.

At the end of June in 1957, my father wrote to his folks to let them know that "Mike's behavior has become progressively worse and more antisocial." Isabelle and Don had asked the Children's Diagnostic Center at Colorado General Hospital to evaluate Mike, and they fully expected him to be committed to residential treatment for his difficult behavior once his name reached the top of the waiting list. Community mental health centers didn't yet exist, and so our family had no affordable alternative that would keep Mike at home.

Dad described Mike's deterioration, which had begun a year earlier. "Mike would sit in the house all day long," he wrote. "I gave him a job of pulling weeds an hour a day just to get him out. He was perverse and resentful of authority."

Halfway through Mike's last school year, Dad reported, his principal called our parents with a heads-up. Mike had become more and more "uncooperative in school and resistant to learning." His outbursts disrupted the class. The principal warned that Mike's "social development was regressing and that we should consider the possibility that he might never be able to take his place in society." By the end of the year, he warned Isabelle and Don that "little time should be wasted."

Mike at 14, in his last class photo, 1957.

Dad wrote to my grandparents, "Mike has withdrawn into himself more and more, and perhaps because of lack of interests, friends, or things to do, he spends his time playing rock-and-roll records or brooding. His behavior is now almost intolerable because of contrariness, defiance, lack of emotional control, and he is a constant agitator, constantly keeping things stirred up."

An outsider might suggest that Mike sounded like a kid on the continuum of standard-issue rebellious teenagerhood. But my brother's agitation moved him beyond that scale of frustrating but acceptable challenges. He was scaring the teachers. At the end of the school year in 1957, the school asked Mom to pick up Mike early each day because even the trained teachers in his special-ed classroom could not control him.

Dad wrote with concern about the state of his family that summer. "Poor Isabelle—she has had to stand this all day long since school was out, and Mike's condition appears to be progressing rapidly."

Our mother had done her best by Mike, but both Don and Isabelle accepted the fact of Mike's illness, his crisis. Denial was not an option.

None of the local institutions could take Mike. Dad had a cousin in Denver, a well-connected doctor who could provide us with an insider's answers. He told our parents that Mike might have to wait another year to get into the treatment system via their applications for help.

And so Don and Isabelle, with the help of the administrators at Mike's school, turned to the only alternative that could generate fast action—a court order requesting immediate psychiatric evaluation, likely leading to institutionalization.

"In a way, this is nothing to feel very bad about," Dad wrote to his folks. "I'm sure that Mike will be much happier in another environment, and it will be much better for the rest of us, too. Mike has been extremely unhappy and has been taking it out on everyone about him. You feel sorry for him at the same time that you can hardly stand to have him around."

Dad laid out the reality facing me when I was six.

No real harm has been done to date, but we feel that a continuation of this atmosphere would be extremely unhealthy for Stevie. He is a remarkably good and well-adjusted child and does a good job of ignoring most of Mike's attempts to stir him up.

The one who suffers most in this is Isabelle. I think Mike literally hates us both now—because we represent the only authority that he must submit to—and it must be terribly hard for her.

Dad was surely right. Anger overwhelmed Mike. His frustration with being categorized as retarded and relegated to special-ed had a new and fiery outlet.

My father had reached the rational conclusion that seeking a court order "provides the best chance for happiness for Mike and for us." His last line: "You needn't worry about Stevie; he's about as fine as you can be."

Maybe I was "fine." Or maybe I was settling into my lifetime of *deciding* to be fine. To be the good son. To block out Mike's difficulties and be an uncomplicated and agreeable and "well-adjusted" guy. I absorbed the possibility that family could disappear, that children could lose their parents. If Mike could be sent away, surely I was at risk, as well, no matter how dependable my parents seemed. Surely these experiences made me a little more accommodating, a little more "good."

OUR HEARTS ARE SORE IN SYMPATHY WITH YOUR SORROW

In his reply to my father's letter, my grandfather lived up to my father's judgment that he was "the nicest man I've ever met." Speaking for himself and for my Grandma Ruby, Grandpa Enoch's answer, typed on letterhead at his big double desk on the screened-in porch of my dad's childhood home, comes from a place of love and empathy.

Dear Son and Daughter, he began.

He described "a real feeling of relief." He reported that Grandma Ruby was so worried she had been unable to sleep past "the real early hours of the morning for some time." He acknowledged that Mike couldn't "fit into our Social Pattern."

Grandpa Enoch lauded Mom's "efforts to bring Mike into the world of reality."

But that was not to be, and he was convinced Mike would be "happier" under the supervision of "trained personnel."

My grandfather—born in 1891, a potato and onion broker with a two-year business college degree—sounded remarkably open-minded in his attitude toward people struggling with their mental health.

We feel that the individual cannot be censored for the deviations from the normal patterns of modern life caused by mental illness. Only the love, attention, and the companionship of happy parents in a real home life prevent some of the tragedies that we read of in the daily papers.

You have given Mike and Stevie the full share of all of these. However, the full and undivided flow of love, attention, and companionship that has been lavished without stint on Mike has failed to light the fire of responsibility to self and others that must be always burning if normal relations with society are to be maintained.

You know that our hearts are sore in sympathy with your sorrow.

Love - Mom and Dad June 23, 1957

In these letters, both men use happiness as a touchstone. And just what is "happiness?" More than the absence of anger and sadness and depression, surely. A word we use to sum up contentment, peace-of-mind, gladness, satisfaction.

What about euphoria, joy? Did Mike ever again experience these exuberant emotions? I suspect he had manic intervals alternating with depression, thrilling highs to counter the black moods. When the doctors diagnosed Mike with schizophrenia, did he hear voices? I so wish I could see my way into his consciousness, penetrate his isolation.

Empathy is the other word hovering everywhere in these exchanges. Dad's empathy for

Mike, for Mom. My grandparents' empathy for all four of us.

As for me, that little boy in the garage, I'm starting from a place where I've walled off Mike's life from my own. Only in the final drafts of this book did I begin to replace "my mother" with "our mother."

I'll need to allow myself to feel my own emotions, not my parents'. I'll need to acknowledge to myself that I'm safe, that I can come in from that metaphorical garage and look around for whatever clues might still exist that will guide me back to my brother.

MIKE IS GONE

In a hearing before the Jefferson County Court Medical Commission at 9:00 a.m. on July 19, 1957, Mike was adjudged mentally incompetent and committed to the Colorado State Hospital. He moved to the mental hospital in Pueblo a week later. He was 14 years old.

Just a month before, on Memorial Day we picnicked in the mountains above Denver, our extended family—Mom, Dad, and me; Mom's sister and her husband; four cousins. And Mike, who was sulky and refused to be photographed. The grown-ups chatted and we kids chased my cousins' dog, Laddie, between the ponderosa pines at Genesee Mountain. Mike hovered on the edges. But he was there. And now, just after the 4th of July, he was gone.

At the hearing, I imagine my parents sat in the courtroom alone, or perhaps with the psychiatrist who evaluated Mike. Mike likely wasn't there. What did our mother say to Mike when she saw him after his commitment? Did she reassure him and tell him that she would see him again soon?

Was Mike so angry that he refused Mom's soothing words? Was he sobbing and afraid, potentially violent, lost to psychosis? Was he too drugged to react?

I fear Isabelle and Don may not have seen him before he was sent off to Pueblo.

Did I have a chance to say goodbye? I would surely miss my brother. And yet I may have felt

more liberation than loneliness, an unspoken gratitude for the sudden harmony at home.

Mike was yanked from his home, held in a psychiatric hospital in Denver for evaluation, and then shipped off to the state hospital in Pueblo for what surely felt like punishment, incarceration. The Jefferson County sheriff likely handcuffed Mike for easy control during the two-hour drive to the state hospital. My brother surely felt bereft—if he wasn't too disturbed to realize what had happened.

Any one of these scenarios would have been harrowing for everyone and likely terrifying for Mike. Mike lost his family. I lost my brother.

I remember nothing.

Facing page: At the family picnic on Memorial Day, 1957, Isabelle looked goofy. Her sister Charlotte vamped for my dad when he looked toward her through the camera viewfinder. Mike refused to be photographed and was caught unawares behind his mother and aunt. I clutched my ball and played with our cousins.

CHAPTER THREE

Today you ruined me.
But have a good summer anyway.
—Mike's letter to Isabelle, June 1, 1967

IF I CAN'T REMEMBER, I can research.
I track Mike's path through the institutional
tangle. I interview mental health professionals
in Colorado. I retrieve the surviving fragments
of Mike's state hospital records, the first new
evidence from Mike's life that I've added to The
Mike File. I feel triumphant, as a writer, and
uneasy, as a brother, as I take these first steps to
bring Mike back from the dead. I don't have a clue
what I'll find.

The hospital documentation begins by de-
scribing newly admitted Patient #38148 by race,
by size, by identifying marks. Mike's record reads
like intake papers for prison.

- *Single Jewish student; age 14; mixed-race.* [The latter, surely a verdict on his ethnic look in that age of lingering anti-Semitism.]
- *5' 11", 141 pounds. Black hair, brown eyes, fair complexion.*
- *Vaccination scar left arm, surgical scar left instep and right instep, surgical scar both legs below knees, scar on left chest.*
- *Environment: Urban.*
- *Education: Common School*
- *Examining doctor: Arcangel*
- *Special precautions: Threatened Mother, little brother & stepfather.*

I imagine disoriented patients hearing that name, "Arcangel," and feeling either reassured by the authority embodied in the name or frantically threatened by its suggestion of absolute dominion. This emissary from the celestial hierarchy welcomes each new arrival to what had been called the Colorado State Insane Asylum until just 40 years before.

When Isabelle and Don first drive the 115 miles south along the base of the Front Range, from Denver to Pueblo, to visit Mike, a heartbreaking amalgam of deliverance, sadness, and guilt must wash over them. They are even more overcome when the aging hospital superintendent, Dr. Frank Zimmerman, tells them not to visit again. "When we admit family members here as a civil commitment, you'd best not visit because that will just disturb them more. It's almost like they are dead to you."

But Mom and Dad keep visiting. Every time I'm dropped off to spend the day with my cousins at my Aunt Charlotte's house in Denver, my mother has to endure her sister's unspoken reproach—or, more likely, snide cuts and jabs—about how Mom has forsaken Mike.

As Mike adapts to his new world, I enter second grade. Our parents want to protect me, but they also want me to maintain as much of a relationship with my brother as possible. So as I get a little older I occasionally go to Pueblo, too.

Pueblo always seemed to me like a place with an edge. The mental hospital folded madness into the city. A steel mill long ruled the economy, attracting the most diverse population in the state. The unchecked power of Pueblo's Colorado Fuel and Iron Company led to the Ludlow Massacre, when the steel mill's security men joined the Colorado National Guard to machine-gun striking miners and their families in 1914, 70 miles south of town. Pueblo had a grittiness that was equal parts exciting and daunting.

I tense and sit up straight in the back seat as we drive into the tree-lined hospital campus. The buildings look haunted. Most of these wards surrounding the grassy quad are stuffed full of long-term patients, quietly spinning out their lives in rocking chairs, the more disruptive residents drugged into calmness by the new pharmacologic wonder, Thorazine. This may be Mike's home, but I know the locked doors hide scenes of out-of-control craziness.

In the long view, Mike's timing was lucky. He just missed the dreadful era when state mental hospitals managed patients suffering psychotic breaks by dulling and traumatizing their brains with massive blasts of electroshock, induced comas, body-chilling hydrotherapy, and lobotomies. I remember hearing that Mike received electroshock treatments—though surely not as intense as the regimen favored a decade earlier.

When Mike was born in 1942, the elite American medical and academic community still supported the pseudo-science of eugenics. Any "feeble-minded" or mentally "defective" person should be isolated, warehoused, neglected, sterilized—maybe even euthanized—to improve the race. In 1935, just seven years before Mike was born, 83 percent of California citizens believed that the mentally ill should be sterilized.

The United States took decades to come around. In 1963, nearly 500 people living in U.S. mental institutions were involuntarily sterilized.

Montana funded a state Board of Eugenics to regulate sterilization of Warm Springs hospital residents until the late 1970s.

World War II was the turning point. When the Nazis used their misplaced faith in eugenics to justify their twisted dream of race purification, a shaken America recoiled. At the same time, thousands of conscientious objectors who completed their service as attendants in American mental institutions came forward after the war to denounce the appalling conditions they had seen in state hospitals—"America's concentration camps." Reform began, finally, and Mike benefitted.

On good days, we take Mike downtown for lunch and to sit for a while in front of the pond and bandstand at Mineral Palace Park. Sometimes when we arrive at the hospital, the doctors tell us that Mike isn't well enough to leave the campus. We walk with Mike under the trees between the institutional red brick buildings. Sometimes the staff tells us that Mike is too ill to see us. Heavy doses of neuroleptic drugs leave patients so lethargic and emotionally indifferent as to be nonfunctional—victims of a "chemical lobotomy."

Other times they tell us Mike is in such terrible shape that they have placed him in restraints—the straitjacket of insane asylum days. Nothing in The Mike File or in the slim hospital records tells me anything more about what his days—or his treatments—were like.

At the end of each visit, we say goodbye, turning away from Mike and back toward our lives in Denver. I don't remember Mike pleading with us to take him home. I remember the partings as calm, but I'm always thankful to leave. Our mother puts on a brave face for Mike and then cries as we drive home, every time.

I try not to look as I listen to my mother grieve, the afternoon sun streaming into the car as we head north back to Denver. I try to become invisible in the back seat. I vow to never make my mother weep like that for me.

THE GEOGRAPHY OF MEMORY

Within a month of Mike's exile from our family, my father headed west for a shortened, delayed field season, beginning a new geologic mapping project in southeastern Idaho. Professionally, Dad had little choice. Still, Mom surely felt deserted. I don't have any letters between them, but I do have Dad's tender postcards to me.

The following summer, in 1958, we left for our first family field season without Mike—where we would spend summers in rented homes in whatever Idaho town lay nearest to Dad's quadrangle

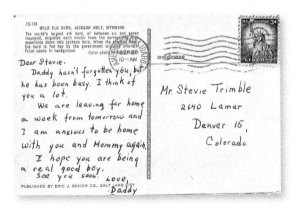

FS-124 WILD ELK HERD, JACKSON HOLE, WYOMING
The world's largest elk herd, of between six and seven
thousand, migrates each winter from the surrounding
mountains down into Jackson Hole. When the snows deep,
the herd is fed hay by the government within this area.
Teton peaks in background. Color photo by ...

Dear Stevie.
  Daddy hasn't forgotten you, but
he has been busy. I think of
you a lot.
  We are leaving for home
a week from tomorrow and
I am anxious to be home
with you and Mommy again,
  I hope you are being
a real good boy.
  See you soon. Love,
                    Daddy

PUBLISHED BY ERIC J. SEAICH CO., SALT LAKE CITY

Mr. Stevie Trimble
2640 Lamar
Denver 15,
   Colorado

assignment until I began college. Each year, we added to a set of experiences Mike could never share.

Our mother took these journeys in stride. Dad's annual summer field seasons removed her from her home and her friends, but they also provided a three-month window of peace, respite from her complicated relationship with her sister Charlotte and the monthly trauma of visits to Mike.

My life just keeps going, from school grade to school grade, from field season to field season. My memories begin to blossom with more detail. I can picture my tiny bedroom in the upstairs apartment we rented in 1958 in Aberdeen, Idaho, oppressive with heat and stuffiness. Our Mennonite landlords lived downstairs. Their teen-aged daughter babysat for me occasionally, and I thought she was cool.

I grow ever closer to our parents during these summers away. We rely on each other, driving to the Grand Tetons for hikes and picnics, accompanied by my dad's running commentary on landscape and western history. We delight in the

Doris Day and Audrey Hepburn movies that play at Pocatello's drive-in theaters.

Mom and Dad had a good time with each other, and I had a good time with them. I had no need yet to separate; their taste was my taste. When my dad was at work, my mom cranked up Frank Sinatra on the stereo, loud. I still know the words to those Great American Songbook standards. The first record album I bought wasn't Elvis but the Henry Mancini soundtrack to the 1962 African adventure film *Hatari!*

I've always accepted the easy reprieve of these summers without questioning. I can see now that I was shaping myself, nurturing and needing family goodwill. I'd seen the turmoil and hurt that Mike had caused. Whether or not I did so consciously, I was becoming the easy child, the easygoing child, not just because of my basic emotional nature but because I needed to be this even-tempered person for our parents' sake.

And what was Mike's life like? He moved to Pueblo just after Colorado Governor Steve McNichols visited the state hospital when he took office in 1957. The governor found "dirty and unsafe buildings and hallways filled with beds—the results of warehousing 6,000 people." He "was actually horrified."

The hospital would have placed Mike first on the men's admission ward, next an active treatment ward, and then a holding ward. Children were housed in separate areas on adult wards. Some daily schooling for these younger kids happened in a dorm on the hospital's dairy farm (with chronic underfunding, the patients raised some of their own food). But as a teenager, Mike would have lived with male patients of all ages, with men who had been institutionalized for decades, coping with every stage of mental illness.

Reading these descriptions, I'm horrified, as well. Mike left Mom's carefully tended home for this ghastly new life. He liked to dress well. He liked to hang around home and listen to music. How could he preserve his identity in these depersonalizing wards full of disturbed men, few of them anywhere near his age?

Governor McNichols initiated a 1958 U.S. Public Health Service survey that found that "costly and careful custodial care" tended to keep patients in the hospital rather than "rehabilitating and returning them to the community." A stay in Pueblo led to "desocialization and chronicity" rather than any chance for former patients to have a go at "productive living."

Reform would come, but frustratingly slowly for anyone like Mike.

THE CARETAKERS

So few clues remain. One tantalizing lead is both ridiculous and riveting. Dariel Telfer wrote a steamy page-turner based on her experiences working at the Colorado State Hospital in the 1950s. The cover blurb for her 1959 book, *The Caretakers*, explains why I stayed up till 2:00 a.m. to finish it: "A shattering novel about nurses, doctors, and patients in a state hospital where emotions readily explode, where lust leads to rape, hate to murder."

In Frank G. Slaughter's review of the book in the *New York Times*, he notes that Telfer's "not a skilled novelist," but he gives her credit for following "the day-to-day life of the hospital with an attention to detail possible only for one who has experienced the things of which she writes. It is not a pretty story, but then the snake-pits of the world are not pretty places."

In Telfer's take on Mike's hospital, life was grim. To set the scene between the overblown scenes of rape, murder, and obsessive infatuation, Kathy Hunter, a nurse in training, gives us her impressions of a male ward—surely just like Mike's ward—that clearly comes from the author's experience in Pueblo:

She entered the ward to find one charge, two attendants, and a huge roomful of men. They were young to middle-aged, one hundred and fifty of them, seated in rows of hard oak chairs. Never had she seen such apathy, she thought, such listless indifference. Some of them rocked slowly and ponderously. Others were immobile, like lifesize carvings. A few stared back at her while others gazed out nearby windows, and a certain number were pushing heavy weights wrapped in pieces of blanket around the floors. This task obviously was designed to keep these patients busy...

The men were allowed no private possessions, no rings, watches, billfolds, photographs, clothing...

...Hour after hour, the men sat in the hard chairs. They shuffled to the toilets and back to the chairs. They drifted to the desk and waited patiently for a light from the matches they were not permitted to carry. ...Sometimes an epileptic would have a convulsion, often hurting himself when he fell during the initial stage and creating mild excitement among the

A photograph from the Colorado State Hospital archives of a crowded men's ward in the 1950s.

attendants, all of which the patients watched pleasurably until the attack subsided. Often there would be quarrels between patients resulting in flailing fists and obscene remarks...

The patients had their own dining room, opened only for the meals which they looked forward to eagerly, not because they were so hungry but because it gave them something to do. When the meal gong rang and the lines began to form, the stronger men pushed and shoved ahead, leaving the feeble and lame and blind for the attendants to guide in. For recreation small groups were taken for strolls on the grounds, but this happened rarely since there were so many men and only four caretakers. However, the men were accustomed to waiting; they were always waiting for something.

...the men slept in dormitories which were kept locked at night. Once each hour, the night shift checked the dormitories, making sure everything was in order. They looked at the beds with flashlights and poked or pulled at covers if something did not seem just right. The patient whose bed was found soiled was in for a bad time.

The smell inside the locked dormitories was terrible, a combination of urine, fecal gas, sweat, and bad breath. Nearly as bad were the combined sounds of groaning, whispering, singing, and cursing. Some of the men tried to get into bed with other men. A few succeeded; others crawled hastily back to their own beds, followed by hoarse shouts of anger.

...She could scarcely visualize them as anything but these lumpish men, when actually they were all sons and some of them were brothers, husbands, and fathers.

Yes, they were. Brothers, indeed.

By the time Joan Crawford and Polly Bergen starred in a 1963 movie version of the book, the script had left behind all that sex and death to morph into a didactic plea for reform. *The Caretakers* was nominated for Best Picture in the Golden Globes, and President John F. Kennedy was so enthralled with the film that he had it screened on the floor of the U.S. Senate, the first movie so honored. The plight of Mike and his fellow patients on their hard oak chairs dramatized in this heavy-handed film energized the president's campaign for community-based mental health treatment in America.

The increasingly liberal Kennedy's passion for reform came directly from his family's experience. Like Mike, JFK's sister Rosemary was diagnosed as mildly retarded as a child and showed psychotic symptoms as a young woman. Determined to find a "cure," her father, Joseph Kennedy, authorized a lobotomy in 1941. Brutally disrupting neuronal connections in an effort to calm her rages, the surgeons left Rosemary shockingly diminished, incapable of speaking. She was institutionalized for the remaining 64 years of her life.

When JFK became president, he vowed to do better. In the first-ever presidential message on mental illness and retardation, followed soon by enabling legislation, Kennedy advocated moving away from the "reliance on the cold mercy of custodial isolation" to "the open warmth of community concern and capability."

Over time, America gutted these programs. The hospitals emptied. Without stable funding for alternative treatment in communities, deinstitutionalization led to epidemic homelessness and incarceration.

Our mental health treatment fails our families even today.

FIVE MILES FROM HOME

From the moment Mike entered the hospital, the state looked for ways to save money and move him back into the community. First, though, the system tried shifting him to Ridge Home, the treatment center for young people with intellectual and developmental disabilities in our suburb back in Denver.

In the few records preserved by the hospital, Mike was deemed "improved" by the summer of 1959, and the staff in Pueblo asked for Mike's transfer to Ridge State Home and Training School. This was breakthrough news—and gave Isabelle and Don hope. Mike's disruptive symptoms must have eased, but the authorities evidently judged his "retardation" significant, requiring residential treatment. The Jefferson County Court issued a change of custody order and Mike moved from the Colorado State Hospital to Ridge at the end of August 1959.

Ridge was close to home, just five miles away. Our mother was thrilled to have Mike for Sunday dinner twice a month. Isabelle was a proud post-war housewife who kept a spotless home, cooked with care, and wanted everybody at the table to enjoy, to laugh, to banter. She was a baker, and we always had homemade cookies and pies. For her, cooking was an act of love.

We spent a lot of time talking during these dinners. Mom delighted in analyzing people, telling stories, trying to figure out her friends. My dad relished arguing about ideas and politics, and he would push, provoke, and play devil's advocate to challenge his dinner companions. When one conservative friend at a dinner party suggested that Richard Nixon wasn't all bad, Dad famously responded, "Neither was Hitler!" Mom was known to kick him under the table when she thought he had gone too far.

Mike didn't say much at these meals. He didn't participate fully even though he surely was desperate for acknowledgment, for his family to understand him. He carried a transistor radio as talisman, his statement of musical taste a shield, a separate identity asserted in the face of our chatter. But he was there, and these visits are the last moments when he might have felt semi-integrated into our family.

Photographs on our front sidewalk are the last pictures I have of Mike—from the fall of 1960, when he was 17 and I was ten. All the animation in these pictures comes from our mother, who looks elated to have her arms around both of her sons. Mike looks resigned, blank, and tall, a totem pole anchored to the sidewalk. Dressed up in my sport jacket, I look self-conscious, a little apprehensive—perhaps trying to fully be the good boy, guided by the polarity between Mike and me like a scatter of iron filings snapped to orderly attention at opposite ends of a magnet.

Mike was sullen on these visits. He didn't say much, and I still found him spooky enough that I didn't ask him questions. I was an ordinary, if nerdy, kid. I had no idea what went on in anyone else's brain, let alone Mike's. The photos remind me of the disturbing Diane Arbus photograph,

"Jewish Giant at Home with his Parents"—the hunched 8-foot-tall Eddie Carmel, looming over his kind, wistful, aging mother and father.

Did Mike feel like he was coming home on these visits? Or had his time in institutions banished any workable definition of home?

In the state hospital, Mike surely began each morning with familiars, with favorites, maybe even with friends. And then the authorities wrenched him away to Ridge. He joined Ridge's classes for high-school-age kids. Like a new kid in any schoolroom, Mike had to make friends in this latest group, a pool of "profoundly developmentally disabled" young people rather than a multi-age group of men with lifetime struggles with mental illness.

Maybe Mike was resilient, after all.

PARALLEL LIVES

Mike moved to Ridge as I began to shape my own life, though it was pretty simple—the life of a nine- to eleven-year-old.

Uneasy with Mike's visits, I surely compensated by being extra sunny, extra perky, extra curious when he was in the house. I was competing with him for my parents' attention, and by any measure, I won that competition.

That first year of Mike's regular appearances at our dinner table, I had a difficult time in school, and perhaps that strange interval was connected to Mike's rejoining our circle. During the first months of fourth grade, our teacher took an extended leave for a major illness. We had a full-time substitute, and I evidently felt free to misbehave without lasting consequences.

I cheated constantly, plucking completed quizzes and worksheets from the pile on the teacher's desk, erasing the name, and writing in my own. I favored Ruby Mayeda's papers because she was smart and because she would be too timid to confront me. I don't remember ever being challenged for this outrageous behavior, though one day on the playground, two boys held me down so that the heftiest girl in our class could punch me for other unknown transgressions.

I also remember stealing—candy bars from the neighborhood drugstore where I was caught once and gently reprimanded by Ernie, the family pharmacist. I stole at school, as well. Tall stacks of *National Geographic* teetered in the corner of the classroom, and I secretly snipped articles I coveted.

Did I act out because of the tension at home? To explain Mom's tiredness on some mornings, Dad later would tell me that she had been walking off her grief in the night, pacing and crying while I slept. Mom hated to reveal "weakness," and I was grateful not to witness her anguish.

After just over two years at Ridge, something different in Mike's behavior, a shift in his brain, an alteration in his neuronal connections, triggered evaluation once again at the Colorado Psychopathic Hospital and "Readmission/transfer" to Pueblo on November 2, 1961.

Penciled into his record was that ominous note, "Special precautions: threatened family." He had left our home with a diagnosis of paranoid schizophrenia, capable of violence. The "precaution" would always follow him.

I've been startled by the murky unfairness of Mike's labels. His doctors were doing their best, but psychiatry was an uncertain science. Half of all mental inpatients in the mid-1950s were diagnosed with schizophrenia—what one psychiatrist of the time recognized later as "a wastebasket" classification.

Average hospitalization after diagnosis lasted 13 years. The state hospital destroyed all the old case files in the 1980s, so I can't know what Mike's therapists said. But in recent decades, psychiatrists have realized that they too often misapplied schizophrenia as a catch-all and consequently misread their patients' needs.

Over and over, the mental health professionals I've spoken with have expressed skepticism about Mike's diagnosis. Many people who had a schizophrenic diagnosis years ago now are judged bipolar, a disorder that surfaced in multiple generations of our family. Mike may well have met the modern threshold for both schizophrenia and bipolar disorder. That would not be unusual; nearly half of people with one mental disorder meet the diagnostic criteria for two or more. We now see mental illness as a spectrum that spans these diseases.

Along the way, Mike developed epilepsy. Perhaps Thorazine triggered his seizures; antipsychotic drugs can have this side effect. His paranoia and dementia might have been more cyclic or transitory than "chronic," more treatable than inescapable. Mike could have been overwhelmed by emotional traumas, anger, umbrage, frustration.

When Mike moved from Ridge Home back to the state hospital, he was two months short of turning 19. He had been institutionalized right through the core of his adolescence. If he had to leave Ridge, he couldn't be doing well. Or perhaps he'd aged out at the "training school" and once he turned 19 was no longer eligible to live there.

But the hospital also felt familiar. Not a home, but a place where people knew Mike and where Mike knew them. I can't make too much of this, since Mike surely yearned to be free of the constraints of his commitment. He lived at the state hospital for another five years. In that interval, Mike lived through the radical transformation of the nation's mental health care.

The hospital had a long way to go. A Pueblo grand jury in 1962 documented abuse and neglect of patients, drunk and unlicensed doctors, hiding places for sex on the grounds, and rampant escapes. The court documented an astonishing 1,345 escapes from January 1961 to March 1962. The hearing acknowledged fear in the citizenry but uncovered no actual crimes committed by patients at large in the community.

Mike had his own adventure away from the hospital grounds when he was 20. He walked away from the state hospital on July 17, 1963. The record reports: "Absent without authority—return urgent." Five days later, the Colorado State Hospital police returned Mike to his ward. I dimly remember hearing that he hung around downtown Pueblo, bored even in this city of 90,000-plus.

In those final years at the state hospital, each year on New Year's Eve Mike celebrated his birthday. He turned 19, 20, 21, 22, 23. Did the staff acknowledge these markers with a celebration, a cake? During the nation's wild ride through the Sixties, I wonder if the wards mourned the loss of President Kennedy or if the draft board kept track of Mike. Did he vote (for even those committed involuntarily don't lose their constitutional rights)? Did he fall in love? Did he make love? It's maddening to know so little.

When I visit the hospital grounds today, I want to stand in front of a ward where Mike lived, I want to stand in his room. But that's impossible. Many buildings have been torn down, others sealed shut with giant sheets of plywood. The place is as eerie as a concentration camp.

Where 6,000 patients lived in 1960, less than 500 live now, mostly "forensic psychiatric patients," convicted psychotic rapists and murderers barricaded behind razor wire by the Department of Corrections at the "Colorado Mental Health Institute at Pueblo." This 21st Century prison for outcasts has erased the geography of Mike's hospital years.

CHAPTER FOUR

You took everything out of my life.
You were never for me since the day I was born.
So leave me alone forever.
–Mike's letters to Isabelle, June 1st and 15th 1967

MIKE'S DEINSTITUTIONALIZATION begins on April 29, 1966, when the hospital issues a 28-day pass to the Halfway House at 10th and West Streets, two miles away on the periphery of downtown Pueblo. And then, three months later, "paroled"—that's the word the administrators use—"on own recognizance to Halfway House," with a drug order to continue treatment.

Schizophrenia was Mike's forever diagnosis. He surely stayed on neuroleptics for the rest of his life, one version or another of Thorazine or Clozapine and their descendants. Unlike treatments for so many other brain diseases, for schizophrenia symptoms, we've never gotten beyond these hard-hitting chemicals that are so tricky to calibrate.

As he takes leave from the hospital, Mike is 23 years old, 6' 1½", and 170 pounds. His records also tell me that he abstains from drinking alcohol. That's all I know about my tall, thin, abstemious brother at this pivotal moment.

He did well in downtown Pueblo. Two and a half months later, in September, he's granted even more freedom when the system "paroles" him considerably closer to our home, to a halfway house on Denver's Capitol Hill.

Mike was the poster child for the new mental health system. No longer confined to a lifelong warehouse for the alone and forgotten, by 1964, two out of three incoming patients were released from Pueblo within a year. Just three weeks after Mike's move to Denver, the American Psychiatric Association bestowed a Silver Achievement Award on the Colorado State Hospital "for its accomplishment in transforming a custodial hospital into a decentralized active treatment facility."

When Mike returned to Denver, Mom first dreamed of release, of Mike free from his demons, of herself free from the encumbrance of his heartbreak. She and Dad and I all imagined that Mike could be incorporated into our lives once more. But none of us understood Mike.

For nine years, he had lived a life we couldn't know. If any of the four of us imagined that he could walk back into the dining room and sit down at the table in the seat saved for him, the same place, the same role, the big brother in our family—his family—we were painfully naive. Isabelle and Don and I had moved forward without him for so long. Mike kept moving, as well, becoming a young adult on his own. Reintegration was going to be challenging for us all.

CHAOS FOR DINNER

Fall 1966. I'm a junior in high school now. I remember being both thrilled and nervous about Mike's return. My high school friends were flabbergasted by his reappearance and disapproving of my silence about his life. One of these buddies couldn't believe I'd never spoken of my brother. He thought I was shockingly cold. He directed his compassion to Mike.

I was ashamed by his accusation. Hadn't I mentioned my brother? But Mike just never came up, and I'd followed my habit of remaining quiet about Mike living off and away in a mental hospital. I repeated my mantras: the story was too complicated, too distant from day-to-dayness. I mimicked my parents' silence.

But while I defended myself only haltingly, I was fierce in my justification of our parents. Mom and Dad had to be right in their decision to commit Mike. They had protected me all these years from the recurring trauma of Mike's journey. Now, I wanted to protect them.

I "love" my explosive brother, but I don't know how to be with him. I have no training, no instincts other than self-preservation. I have a hard time looking him in the eye. Mike is a stranger. Mike is strange.

He rides the city bus out to our suburban neighborhood frequently for dinner. Dad picks him up at the end of the line, a mile away. Mike brings chaos with him—or the *potential* for chaos. His physical and emotional stature overwhelm our little house. Neither my father nor I make it to 5′ 8″, and Mom is 5′ 4″. To us, Mike is huge.

But this is my chance to know my brother. I'm old enough, he's open enough. He's fully alive and puts out a lot of energy, all of it unfamiliar. I remember his presence as intense, loaded, though I can't quite get to the content of what he said. Still, these memories capture the most vivid version of Mike I have. He's loud, talking assertively, with jagged modulation. He's craving reconnection, but I'm still scared of him, and I'm sure he senses this. I withhold. I observe. The bond can't form—or reform.

Our awkwardness around him makes things worse. We love books and politics, Mike does not. He is volatile, Mom and I are conflict averse. I don't ask Mike to tell me stories. I fear the content of the answers. So I revert to the habitual repartee I have with our parents—running jokes, wordless understandings, favorite foods, years of road trips and stories, none of which Mike can share, even if we try to include him in the conversation.

Of course Mike feels unwelcome. He has no coping skills. We fail in our puny efforts to validate him, to accept him for who he is, to show real interest.

In this new life outside the hospital, Mike tries a sequence of jobs—working in laundries, wiping down vehicles at a car wash. Nothing works out, the jobs too rigid in expectation and schedule, the dinners Mom prepares with hope and tenderness undermined by Mike's frustration and alienation.

Within weeks, Mike realizes that he can't handle these dinners. He tries one last time at Thanksgiving, but storms out before the meal, walking to the bus stop and into his own life. I can still feel the whirlwind of anger and disappointment that envelops him as he slams the door.

Mike cannot pick up where he left off, no matter how much we all long for him to do so. We have too much history and too little understanding. He brings too much resentment. Mike needs more emotional room than we know how to give. He can't penetrate our threesome after nine years away. And we do not know how to accept him as the young man he's become.

LISTEN I LOVE YOU
AND ALL THAT BUT STILL

A few months later came the summer of heart-rending letters that Mike wrote to our mother while my parents and I were living in Idaho for Dad's field season. I remember Mom telling my father at the end of a day when he came home from walking the hills in search of slaty argillite and basin-and-range faults, his clothes laced with the acrid bittersweet of sagebrush, "Another letter came."

Mom was devastated by the hurtfulness of Mike's words. I was self-involved.

At 16, I had my first paying jobs. Every Sunday evening, I played French horn in the Pocatello Municipal Band, gleefully pocketing $8 for showing up at the Ross Park bandshell to *oom-pah-pah* in the Sousa marches. At the end of each weekday, I clocked in at Woolworth's on Main Street for a couple of hours to pry off wads of gum and sweep and mop the aging linoleum floors. I spent the rest of my time at the Supersonic Car Wash, reading fat James Michener and Leon Uris novels while waiting for the line to get busy enough for the foreman to ask me to punch in and help. For a brief time that summer in our respective cities, Mike and I were both wiping down cars.

While I was piecing together money sufficient for a teenager's luxuries, Mom was figuring out how to respond to Mike's letters.

She saved all of Mike's scrawling pages, an act of grit and courage. They are the most demanding items preserved in The Mike File. I don't know how she read them once, let alone returned to them. Except for a few glances, I've quarantined them until now. I want to bring to bear all that I've learned about our mother and my brother when I give the letters their due.

I have seven letters from Mike addressed to our mother, two from Mike to our aunt Charlotte. I'll transcribe them as Mike wrote them, without changing spelling or syntax, without fixing or flagging his missing words. I've put them in sequence, from June 1st to July 5th. Mike starts off with a bang.

Thursday, June 1, 1967.
To Mom:

Listen I love you and all that but still you should have realized what you did wrong to yourself and me. You made some of the worst mistakes that any mother should ever make. You took everything out of my life. ...
Why don't you admit to yourself what you did wrong.

...because you didn't get anything out of your life when you were a child you wanted to take and mess your own son's life up entirely. Well, I'll tell you did a darn good job of it. ...I don't want to ever hear from you or the Stepdad. You better leave me alone entirely from know on out. I mean business.

You think I am a fool. I am lot smarter than you put me on to be. ...You people are sick, selfish, and very unfair. I will send you people something for rememberance. ...I'd been better off in an orphanage after I was born because you sure didn't deserve me one bit.

...So leave me alone forever. I am just sorry you deprived me of everything. Because if I had Good Frame Peace of Mind I'd probably in business for myself. Today you ruined me. But have a good summer anyway.

Love, Mike

Mike's letters swing back and forth (perhaps, one psychologist friend suggests, with the oscillating levels of his meds)—from these insistent "leave me alone forever" cries of frustration to apologies and best wishes. Both extremes are equally plaintive. The words are confused and angry and sad.

In her essay, "The Empathy Exams," Leslie Jamison suggests that you "enter another person's pain as you'd enter another country, through migrations and customs." These letters take me into Mike's unfiltered pain. I am appalled that until now I've spent so little energy seeking to enter his country, his landscape of ache and frustration. But I'm here now. Each time I read Mike's words, I feel gut-punched. And I wonder at the astonishing fact that I've never before visited this emotional realm where Mike lived his days.

Scholar and storyteller Brené Brown gives me another window on empathy, which she equates with self-compassion. "Empathy is the antidote to shame," she says. "If you put shame in a petri dish, it needs three things to grow exponentially. Secrecy, silence, and judgment. If you put the same amount of shame in a petri dish and douse it with empathy, it can't survive."

To have a relationship with Mike, to be truly present for him, I would have needed a set of tools and skills I clearly lacked. The tools I did employ involved compartmentalizing and numbing. I didn't aim for secrecy, but silence and secrets dwell together. Judgment followed.

Platitudes abound. "That was then, this is now. Your parents took the lead. You couldn't have acted then the way you could today. You can't judge your youthful self from the righteous platform of hindsight." And so on.

The fact remains, I was accustomed to life without Mike. It was surely easier to return to that predictability when he cut himself off from our family, his family. In the letters of mine that our mother saved—dozens of letters from 1968, when I left home for college, right through Mike's death in 1976 and onward—I never mention him, never ask about him, never acknowledge his existence in any way.

Brené Brown articulates the tragedy of all this for Mike. "We are psychologically, emotionally, cognitively, and spiritually hard-wired for connection, love, and belonging. Connection… is what gives purpose and meaning to our lives."

AND SO...

No matter how loving our mother's intentions, no matter how compassionate my father, how could Mike not bristle at his long years in the hospital? He had an intellectual disability, but he was not oblivious.

Without much pondering, I had always assumed that Mike spent these years consumed by his illness, drugged or delusional, his life and thoughts circumscribed by his wayward brain. But his psychosis was not constant. There would have been times when he wasn't paranoid, when he was his best self, when he felt outrageously misplaced. These letters reveal that he spent many hours and days and years imagining his lost life, feeling homesick, angry, rejected, abandoned.

In the letters, Mike refers icily to Don as "the Stepdad," though I remember him using "Dad" when he was with my father. Mike harbors remarkably little antipathy towards me, generally including a "Say hello to Steve." But he envies my featured role. He surely felt his banishment as a pronouncement of failure. He saw Don and Isabelle cherish me. "You treat Steve like the cream of the crop and you treat me like a no good for nothing nut. You are very unfair..... You think Steve's the greatest. But to you and your side of the family, I am just a big louse and no good."

Don and Isabelle reveled in my success and surely believed that I owed some of my accomplishments to their decision to protect me from the grief and hopelessness of Mike's story. I've always thought of myself as a person with minimal angst, but how much of my even nature was shaped in response to Mike, a subconscious striving for contrast? Mike was erratic; I was compliant. Mike was hard; I was flexible. Now, I realize I need to insert "and so" into each of these sentences.

Mike's reference to "your side of the family" distinguishes our nuclear family from Mike's aunt and uncle, Mom's sister Char and her husband, Harry. Mike identified with Charlotte's flair and Harry's flaunting of his comparative wealth. Mike didn't connect with Don's disinterest in business and passion for science. Charlotte and Harry didn't connect with my dad for the same reasons, and never knew what to make of me, a bookish kid with no interest in sports or business.

Don's family was not Jewish. Though thoroughly small-town, the Trimbles included schoolteachers, doctors, and librarians sprinkled through the small businessmen and farmers who mostly made up their extended clans. In contrast, all four of Mike's biological grandparents came from Orthodox Jewish families, making their way in retail and trade. Maybe Mike's immigrant entrepreneurial heritage prevailed. He wrote to Mom, "your husband knows my interests as a kid and in previous years are just never were in his field. So that the things he tried to teach I just not care to do. I am altogether a much different than anybody would ever want on your side of the family."

When Mike apologizes, he means it—in the moment. "I realize my faults and some of the crazy stunts I pulled in the past and lot of it was just uncalled for."

Some of his protests come from knowing at some deep level that our mother loves him, and so he keeps returning to his astonishment at her complicity in his commitment. His accusations feel both just and unfair. To some of my psychologist friends, the impulsive emotional wrenching in his letters feels more like the intense sensitivity of borderline personality disorder than schizophrenia.

WHAT I WOULD HAVE BEEN

Mike tries to explain to Mom how the doctors got things wrong. He doesn't believe in question marks or commas and joggles his words, but any of us can lose ourselves in fiery tangles of syntactical detours when we are upset.

You see Mom these Dr.'s are set so well that they just told you wrong things about me. I am not fibbing to you. You can say well they are Proffessionals from your own bystanding. ...You see Mom they will you anything to make money because a lot of this is just a racket anyway. Know for instance when you me both they just told you that I was this way and you believed.

...I was never an M.R. like everybody thought I was. In fact, some of the ones told from down at the hospital thought I never was in the first place. Did you know why I went to the State Home out in your neck of the woods. At the time not because of them but because of a misunderstanding of different people under a different administration at the time. I topped everything in that home. I was smarter than [all?] of them... I hope that someday you will realize what I would have been if you wouldn't have messed me up.

The State Home was Ridge State Home and Training School, where Mike spent those two years closer to us, and where Mike *was* smarter than anyone else there, all those "M.R.s" branded with the diagnosis of profound "mental retardation."

Mike was looking back at his life, at us, at me, fully aware of his loss, resentful of our moving on and leaving him behind. I'd given him no recognition for such perfectly predictable and natural feelings. And in many ways, he was right about his institutional doctors. They knew little and yet acted decisively, casually institutionalizing people for decades.

In the attack letters where Mike insists he'll never see our mother again, he tells her that his therapists have encouraged him to make the break.

My counselor told me down in Pueblo to stay away from you all because of the fact that we do not get along and we argue. The hospital even told me before I left down there, Mike live your own life and let your Folks live theirs. ...not that I don't to see you again but it is the best thing for all of us because you know get up upset and just doesn't or never did work or never will. ...It was alright when I was a kid but know I am much older and I have a lot of proving to do on my behalf. Don't think that I still don't like you to a certain extent because I do but I have to stay away from you all of what has happened to me.

The People in Rehab told me to stay away from you altogether once in for all. You are a troublemaker. Actions speak louder than words. You make me upset and you never meant well by me anyway.

Line after line in Mike's letters pierced our mother to her core. Mike's accusations played on Isabelle's guilt. She would have to wonder, maybe those psychiatrists who blamed mothers for their children's schizophrenia were on to something.

"You never loved from the start. You messed my life around."

"Don't bother to write to me no more or don't bother to get in contact with me either. I've disowned you forever."

"You have doubted my abilities and what I could do. You didn't realize a good son when you had me."

"Don't ask me to come out for Thanksgiving either or any other time because I won't show up. I am only welcome in your home so Don and you can hurt my feelings."

"As far as I am concerned you have failed as a Mother on my part. You will have to do without me for the rest of your life."

I read these letters and think first of our mother reading them. The letters let me *see* Mike, but first I see our mother, reading and responding and raw. My empathy goes first to her.

Isabelle had many reasons for saving the letters. A sense of their importance to her, to Mike.

The record they constitute of Mike's self, his for-
midable emotional presence. They carry universal
value, too. I think Mom knew they were too powerful to simply toss in the rubbish bin after a first,
painful, hurried read. Even if you didn't know the
writer or recipient, their outpouring of confusion
and pain deserve the dignity of preservation, the
permanence of The Mike File.

LIVE, LEARN, FORGET

When I read in Mike's letters, "I am a person with
great determination, power, desire, initiative, and
confidence in myself to make in this big revolving
world. I am fighter to the end," I ache for him. In
a life that leaves him diminished and embittered,
he's looking for ways to recover his self-esteem.
He clearly thought about missed opportunities
and, in a kinder world, not all of his daydreaming
would have been far-fetched. He knew, he *knew*,
that his twin disabilities shouldn't have destroyed
his options so completely.

In one letter, Mike quoted "a philosopher in Ancient history" who once said, "live, learn, and forget." Mike repeats the phrase in several letters. Somehow he connects the resonance of that phrase with Judy Garland in *A Star is Born*. He writes to our mom, "She reminds of what I could have been if you wouldn't have messed me around."

Why that 1954 movie? Had Mike seen it on television? Mike may have somehow linked the movie to his affinity with our aunt Charlotte, who adored Judy Garland's singing. Garland's addictions and suicide attempts were legendary when Mike wrote these letters. Her biographers suggest that she may well have had a mental illness herself, a borderline personality disorder. So Mike may have seen her as someone like him overcoming disability to achieve success and fame.

In *A Star Is Born*, Garland's character becomes a major celebrity after her discovery by James Mason, who plays the alcoholic actor who falls in love with her. At the peak of her stardom, she offers to give up her career to caretake her lost-soul husband who created that career "by his faith and by his love."

When I watched the film—all three hours of the full-length 1983 restoration—I could imagine Mike dreaming of a caretaker or even a partner for himself. Garland's character says of her wayward husband, "Maybe if I'd had a chance to be with him more, some of these things wouldn't have happened."

Or was there some connection to Judy Garland as a gay icon? One cousin remembers Mike as effeminate and guessed he might be gay. Like so much of Mike's life, I can neither reject nor verify her hunch.

In the movie's finale, James Mason's troubled character walks into the ocean to drown. Mike's biological father, Morey Sher, would take his own life just three years after Mike wrote these letters. I know I'm staring into a fun-house mirror distorting bits and pieces of Mike's life and dreams.

THE "REAL DAD"

When Mike returned to Denver in his mid-twenties, he looked up his "Real Dad," his biological father. Morey Sher's rejection was devastating. When Mike wrote to Mom and Char about the brief experience, his tone changed from rage to yearning. Here are the letters, in full, written on the eve of the birthday our mother shared with her younger sister.

Thursday, June 29, 1967

Dear Char

Want to wish you a Happy Birthday. I wonder if you want to give me another chance. I found out you were right and Mom was right. Me and my Real Dad's relationship did not work out it went on the rocks as of tonight. He doesn't want anything to do with me no more. He doesn't want to see me. I am lonely and I need somebody to talk to. You can call me if you like

at 377-8213. *Have good celebration Saturday night.
Of course you always do. Happy 40 tomorrow.*

*I was kind of afraid this would happen and it did.
I am willing try to get along with you that much more
know. Also true what I said. If I can be given another
chance I'll try just the much harder now. With love,
your nephew Mike Say hello to everyone for me.*

Thursday, June 29, 1967

Dear Mom

*How are you? Happy Birthday tomorrow. I have
considered our relationship as of going back together
again and I'll tell you why. You know that between
the 2 of us we had a lot of misunderstandings and
misleadments as of what happened to me throughout
my life. You know have suffered terribly in this world
through a world of loneliness a lack of things that the
Proffesssionals weren't sure about when they told you
what my case history was at birth and through the
previous years of life. I overcame and sold myself on
that. You know it hasn't been easy throughout my life.*

Dear mom   Thursday
June 1967
How are you? Happy
Birthday tomarrow
I have considered
our relationships
of going back together
again and I'll tell
you why. You know
that between the 2
of us we had a lot
of misunderstandings
and misleadings
of what happened
to me throughout
my life. You know
have suffered terribly
in this world living
a world of loneliness
a lack of things that
the Proffesionals
weren't sure about
when they told you
what my cat has by
was at birth

Well, I'll tell you it's up to you whether or not you want to see me again after all the wrong things I said about you. I want to see you again when you come back in September. Well you said there is always 2 sides of the story and you are so right on that my Real Dad disowns as of tonight. I hadn't seen him in 6 weeks. Sent him a Fathers Day card and even wrote to him and tried to please him and know he will have nothing to do with me whatsoever. It wasn't really worth the time and trouble to get him back in contact with him so far as our relationship was concerned. Now I see why you divorced him. He does not care for me and you were right all the time but I had to learn the hard way. I seen him often and on for 32 days and that was all. Out of not seeing him in all my life.

Let's learn, live, and forget get back on the right tract again if we can. You'll try and I'll try it if you want to. It's up to you. If you'll give me another, I'll give you another chance, so far as your relationship is concerned. Think it over and write to me if you want to. A far as my meals and rent are coming along, it's alright. I am getting by in this big deep revolving world. Tell everyone hello for me. I mean out of the sincereness of my heart.

I send Char some candy rosebud mints for her birthday yesterday. Also a card. Payed postage and everything, the works. So if you reconsider me will write to each other again. Let me know now. I am a very lonely person. So Happy 46 tomorrow. Have a good celebration. Love, Mike

P.S.. Write soon if you want. Say hello to Steve for me.

For a moment, our mother seemed like a beacon of understanding. She cared, and Mike knew it. But by the next week, he was back to declaring his need to be independent. He wrote two last letters, one to Isabelle and one to Charlotte. And those are the last of his words that I have.

To Mom, "Don't even come and see me no more. ...I know all the answers and you've tried to judge and doubt my abilities and everything. So don't bother me. I mean business. I am not what you thought I called for birth. Take a trip to Montana or Utopia.

I can't care less where you go or what you do. I am of age now so I don't have to listen to what you are Don says to me."

To Char, *"…Just rip my telephone number up and my address. You make me upset and miserable because that Mother of mine I have to make my own life as I see it not as you or she sees it. Everybody else is alright. I am just a worthless piece of junk.*

…I am sorry it had to end this way…I like you personally but I am better off to stay away from all of you once and for all. It's unfair and unjust. You tell that Mother and Stepdad to stay away from me to. Tell her not to come to see or to call me either. She is the one broke me and my Real Dad's relationship. She is the blame for what all has happened… Love Mike"

Mike's "real dad" could have unlocked the door to another family. The Shers could have reached out. I've searched for them and met them. They are kind people; Morey Sher was an anomaly in his clan. He never allowed his family to embrace his son, denying Mike a reservoir of potential love and support.

The man's behavior was consistent. When Mom filed for divorce in 1943, just five months after Mike's birth, the divorce papers reported that Sher "has been extremely and repeatedly cruel," inflicting both "mental suffering and bodily violence."

Twenty-three years later, did Mom's first husband still resent her departure from their marriage? I can imagine his regret at having a child, his guilt, his embarrassment and shame about his son's mental illness and developmental disabilities. Or was Morey Sher just self-involved? The surviving Shers can't answer these questions for me. No one can.

Learn, live, forget.

I'm not sure what any of us learned, but Mike lived for another nine years.

And I continued to be a master of forgetting.

CHAPTER FIVE

I am a person with great determination, power, desire,
initiative, and confidence in myself.
I am getting by in this big deep revolving world.
—Mike's letters to Isabelle, June 6th and 29th 1967

YOU STEP FROM YOUR CAR, distracted, headed for an appointment. A homeless man approaches. Bearded, unkempt, wild-eyed. You know you should be empathetic, but he comes too close. No sense of boundaries, no filters, jumpy in his movements. You pull back, you stiffen, on alert, expecting a request for a handout or a disorganized rant about lurking CIA operatives.

You feel guilty, but you don't want to get drawn into messiness. You nod, you smile tightly. You look away. You move on.

Mike may have had some of this look of The Other, even if I remember him cleaner, better dressed, and better groomed than most of the people we see walking on downtown sidewalks, conversing in erratic outbursts with unknown listeners. Most of us turn away from these people in need, no matter how forlorn they seem. We don't want to get involved.

Mike never retreated from his painful decision to cut off contact with us. We honored his appeal to be left alone. And he wasn't the only returning patient to lose connections with family. The vast majority of people released from the state hospital did not return home. They had no families to take them in.

The Galvins were an exception. In this tragic and astonishing family—so vividly described in Robert Kolker's 2020 book, *Hidden Valley Road*—ten of the twelve children are boys, and six of these boys are diagnosed with schizophrenia. They live in Colorado Springs. Beginning in 1970, they cycle between the state hospital and their home throughout their lives. "Pueblo" carries the same weight in their family as in ours. But the Galvin brothers lived in a new era of care that rejected warehousing patients for decades. The family was determined to keep them in their circle—a fierceness built from both love and denial.

In Mike's day, nearly everyone leaving the hospital in Pueblo ended up in halfway houses, boarding houses, or, eventually, on the streets. In Colorado, the community-based services needed for effective housing and treatment couldn't cope with the flood of patients migrating out of Pueblo. With time, resources grew ever more scarce.

Coming to Denver "paroled" as an ex-state hospital patient, Mike carried nearly the same stigma he would have endured if he'd been released from prison. The language we use to describe people like Mike matters. We react differently to "retarded and schizophrenic" than we do to "people with intellectual disabilities and psychiatric illness."

When I was a kid, one way to cope with my brother's banishment was to picture Mike living in the best possible situation for someone like him, a sort of boarding school, a place he accepted, adapted to, maybe even preferred. After he left the hospital and cut himself loose from us, I could imagine him as an independent actor, with a circle of similar folks to hang out with. But I never visualized details. I had no starting point.

Meanwhile, I took my peaceful and privileged life with our parents for granted. I acknowledged my brother just once a year. At least through high school, I sent Mike presents for Christmas and for his New Year's Eve birthday. Aftershave. A carton of cigarettes. He sent a brief thank you. And then I returned to my classes, my friends, my enthusiasms, giving him no thought, sometimes for months.

The final diagnosis in Mike's chronology at discharge in spring 1967 brands him with a lifetime label, "Schizophrenic reaction, residual type." The patchy record makes no mention of "retardation." Psychiatric disorder evidently trumped intellectual disability. The very last line marks his official discharge from the hospital in October 1967, a year after his arrival in Denver: "Condition, Improved—Administrative Discharge."

How "improved" was he? What happened to his "schizophrenia?" Controlled? No reports from Pueblo can tell me. And Denver General Hospital has no files from outpatients who used their services so long ago. The record lists two last Capitol Hill addresses with October dates. And that's it. Mike disappears.

LET IT BE

On a cold winter-gray day in 1970, I drive through downtown Denver in our inelegant old pinkish-tan 1962 Dodge Dart, the family car now passed on to me. I'm home from college on winter break, running errands. Multi-lanes of traffic carry me down Broadway, through the heart of the city, the heart of the state. The Capitol rises to my left, its gold dome incandescent in low-angled light. Off to the right, khaki-colored grass leads past leaf-less black branching trees reaching skyward, the imposing Civic Center behind. Steam plumes from vents. The breath of the city.

A line of people stands on the curb, bundled up for winter, waiting, watching, or maybe just killing time. And there's Mike, at the front of a cluster of folks at a bus stop. He wears that same scowl of unhappiness I remember. He's a slouching column of dark tallness, a cigarette dangling from his fingers.

I slow down, I grip the wheel, hesitant, agitated, but can't quite get myself over to the curb. I want to stop. I'm scared to stop. My AM radio blasts The Beatles—*The Long and Winding Road that leads me to your door...* and *Let It Be.* Conflicting advice. No help there.

I'm riveted to Mike as I roll by. He doesn't make eye contact. Even if he saw me, he might not recognize me. Mike wanted nothing to do with us, right? What in the world would I say?

I don't pull over, roll down the window, call to him.

Before I know it, I'm past, still clutching the wheel. I do not drive around the block to give myself a second chance to push through my uncertainty, stop, park, hop out of the car, and catch Mike before he moves on, boards his bus, disappears. I let the current of traffic carry me downstream, south along Broadway, away from my brother.

My recollection of this encounter *moves*, like a scene from a movie, a YouTube video clip. It's one of those permanent memories generated when you lock onto a scene, staring so hard at someone or something that there's a taut line carrying the image right into your brain where it remains forever vivid.

After so many years of Mike existing as an abstract fact in the nether reaches of reality, without detail or motion, this chance sighting of my brother takes on the full resonance of regret. I remember the moment with utter clarity because I'm so mortified by my failure to call out to him. I simply don't have the confidence, the empathy, the kindness, the agency, to stop.

I saw Mike one additional time, walking across a street in downtown Denver as I drove by. Again, I didn't stop. I'm surprised I didn't run into him more often. Denver hadn't hit its big growth spurt in these years. It still felt like a small city, but not small enough for Mike and me to cross paths frequently on my visits home.

HEROES IN THE ALMSHOUSE

We had no contact with Mike for nearly ten years. In that decade, I matured, slowly. I celebrated birthdays from 16 to 26. I won a scholarship to college; traveled as far as Europe, Israel, South America; became a mountaineer, a park ranger; began grad school; published my first small pieces of writing, with my photographs. With one weak eye and no depth perception, I escaped the Vietnam-era draft despite my low lottery number. I was on my way to what most would call the normal adulthood of a privileged straight white male.

Mike always maintained his distance, though he accepted small checks from our mother for spending money. He never contacted our parents or me about a visit. Did he sometimes consider a call or waver in his ferocity? The 1967 letters show agonizing ambivalence. Did our parents try to break through his barriers? I know I did not.

Mike still came into my Uncle Harry's downtown Denver jewelry store occasionally. He wrote to Charlotte. He reached out to his aunt and uncle, who hadn't sent him to the state hospital.

Mike admired Char and Harry. They cultivated an aura of affluence. They were embedded in Denver's Jewish business community. They weren't his parents. Mike couldn't have picked up a strong Jewish identity from our adamantly anti-organized-religion mother, but he might have *chosen* to think of himself as Jewish to locate himself in a world closer to his aunt.

Mike's quiet life in Denver could have been a function of his disabilities, his illness, his childhood trauma. External forces didn't help. Paternalistic boarding home operators and the dependable arrival of disability checks encouraged passivity and idleness. And years on numbing neuroleptics have a permanent deadening effect. Psychotropic drugs save lives, but when I read writer and activist Robert Whitaker, he emphasizes the wrenching trade-off: "...people who tolerated neuroleptics well, and weren't 'relapsing,' were living purposeless, isolated, and largely friendless existences."

My father maintained remarkable empathy for his troubled stepson throughout these years. Mike's life sparked my father's evolution from small-town Republican to passionate believer in the Democrats' societal safety-net. Dad had rejected his family's conventional Christianity long ago in grade school. But he didn't move on from the conservative politics he grew up with until he experienced Mike's struggles. As he later explained to anyone who would listen, especially his least progressive friends, we can't all pull ourselves up by our bootstraps. For the rest of his life, Dad told this story as the parable that redefined his political identity.

His tutorial went like this. Mike was born needing help from his community. I was born eight years later, securely holding the world by the tail. Mike came with a history that set him apart, and society was ready to brand him a failure and sideline him as a threat. I came with a stable emotional baseline and workable intelligence.

This chasm between possibilities, and the need to compassionately address that gap, turned Dad into a progressive, a social liberal. Through all the tumult of America's next fifty-five years, he only grew more disgusted with our abandonment of those in need. In his nineties, he emphatically described himself as a "radical Democrat."

Mike logged his nine years of confinement at the hospital and emerged with his discharge certificate, "improved." He returned to Denver and lived on his own for another ten years. And yet society has trouble thinking of him as a fellow citizen and community member who happens to have a brain that works differently. No one ever described him as a young man who demonstrated real bravery when he faced each new day.

He must have spent these years in group homes (also called board-and-care homes), "the modern version of the almshouse…a community-based back ward," as writer and therapist Ann Braden Johnson puts it.

Mike wasn't so much deinstitutionalized as reinstitutionalized for his last decade. Federal welfare covered his board and room and a bit of spending money. Cigarettes, a movie. Bowling, perhaps. Medicaid covered his drug expenses and whatever therapy he received.

Minimally licensed, group homes had one primary mission, to make money for the owner. Apart from a brief interlude of well-funded follow-up care, Mike went from warehoused inmate to commodity. Neither role gave much thought to his humanity or his needs. President John F. Kennedy's plan for federally funded community mental health treatment hadn't worked sustainably for Mike and his peers. They remained mostly on their own.

LOVE, WORK, PANCAKES

A widely-quoted aphorism from Freud tells us that "Love and work are the cornerstones of our humanness." Mike, as far as I know, had few avenues for either.

As I try to conceive of Mike's happiness, how he structured his life to meet his needs as best he could, I think of *Rain Man*. Mike wasn't Raymond Babbitt, the Rain Man so memorably acted by Dustin Hoffman, and I'm not Charlie, the arrogant hotshot younger brother played by Tom Cruise. But Charlie spends a week with his *savant* brother on their memorable road trip and makes "a connection." That experience transforms their relationship. Charlie, self-involved and selfish, for the first time can say of Raymond, the brother he had forgotten, "This is my family."

At the end of the movie Charlie harangues Raymond's doctor. "Did you spend 24 hours a day, seven days a week with him? Have you ever done that? When we started out together, he was only my brother in name. And this morning... we had pancakes. I made a connection."

It never occurred to me to seek out Mike, for pancakes, for connection, for anything at all. His place in my life was defined by a rote explanation whenever I got around to mentioning him. The best I could muster was to add new phrases to my mantra as Mike added new chapters in his life.

"I have a retarded brother—a half-brother. He left home when I was six when he was swept away by schizophrenia. He spent years at the state hospital and now lives in a halfway house and wants nothing to do with our family."

His existence barely mattered to me in these years. But his existence always mattered to our mother.

So did his death.

CHAPTER SIX

You will have to do without me for the rest of your life.

—Mike's letter to Isabelle, June 16, 1967

ONE THURSDAY in December 1976, my cousin Cathy—Charlotte's oldest daughter, 28 at the time—stops by my parents' house to have dinner. Isabelle gets to cook for someone she loves, and Cathy gets a good meal and a ration of affection from her aunt and uncle in between her daytime stint of teaching junior high English and an evening of parent-teacher conferences.

As Cathy walks up the short curve of sidewalk to our front door, she reaches down and snags the afternoon paper, *The Denver Post*. She pops off the rubber band, unfolds the front page, and prepares to lay the paper on the black faux-leather hassock just inside the door where each day the news launches its journey through our family.

A headline at the top of Page One catches her eye:

Death Knocked...but Only Mike Was Listening

Cathy glances at the first few lines. The *Post* reporter, Patrick McGuire, opens with,

Sometime last Friday night or early Saturday morning, Michael Trimble, 33, slipped through one of those cracks The System is so famous for.

Cathy keeps reading, her eyes widening, her throat constricting, as she walks into the kitchen where my mother is making dinner and my father mixing the nightly gin-and-tonics. The news story goes on.

He died, all alone in his squalid room at the Carefree Guest Home—a licensed personal-care boarding home which is supposed to supervise invalids like Mike Trimble who are too disabled to live alone.

But it wasn't until a maid went into Trimble's room late Monday morning, more than two days after his death, that anyone at the Carefree Guest Home knew Mike was dead.

Dumfounded, Cathy realized that her aunt didn't yet know. This front-page story would inform Isabelle that her son was gone—in dramatic, public, heartsinking detail.

I will think of my brother in a moment. I will. But first I picture the scene in our kitchen, our mother's new reality. The three crowded together in shock, Don or Cathy reading aloud, the description of Mike's "squalid" room. Isabelle, rapidly crumpling. The chronology of Mike's last moments in a reporter's spare language.

Was Mom able even to hear the words after the first few lines?

The next few paragraphs took the three further into Mike's experience.

On Friday evening, December 10th, my brother told Richard Clark, who operated the Carefree Guest Home where Mike lived in Denver's West Highland neighborhood, that he would be staying with friends that weekend. Clark made no point of telling anyone working at the guest home that Mike planned to be away. Mike climbed the stairs to his second-floor room and closed his door for the night. Clark didn't give Mike a second thought.

No one, it turned out, gave Mike a second thought.

One staff member reported seeing him at breakfast early Saturday morning. But when that maid finally went into Mike's room late Monday morning, she was startled to find Mike still in bed. Startlement quickly turned to distress. Mike's corpse already was decomposing.

In our kitchen, "I don't remember what happened next, exactly," Cathy told me. "But Isabelle was horrified. I felt awful, because I was the bearer of bad tidings, even though it didn't have anything to do with me. Isabelle was gone the rest of the night, pacing.

"She was completely shielded in a bubble, and that's all she could deal with, all she could think about." Cathy remembers the experience as "earth-shaking." Cathy felt Mike's life and death left "a permanent hole" in my mother's heart with impacts both conscious and unconscious.

ROOMS FULL OF ANGUISH

Mom and Dad telephoned me. Feeling heartsick but detached about Mike, I drove the 900 miles from Tucson, where I was in graduate school. As my truck rattled along, I wondered how I could possibly help my mother.

I had lost Mike. In some deeply buried place, I was afraid I would lose my mother, as well.

I pulled in to our driveway, walked through the cold night air, and opened the door to my childhood home. What had always been the setting for Mom's delight in cooking and storytelling with my visiting friends had lost its light-hearted soul. My dad was bleak with concern for my mother. My mom was still pacing the short run of our house between bedroom and kitchen.

Over the nearly 20 years since Mike's commitment to the mental health system, Isabelle may have rationalized some of her despair, but this public trumpeting of Mike's lonely death was too much for her. Our little house couldn't contain her suffering. Her anguish filled the rooms.

My mother's ocean of loss and guilt and mourning overwhelmed her capacity for words. She swept back and forth in her robe, gripping a wadded Kleenex, a King Lear-like groan of frustration and misery punctuating every few steps. I knew she hated for anyone to see her in this state, so there was mortification in these heaving sighs, too. My father's tenderness for her, his grounding, his voice of reason, did nothing to calm her. And all the while, we lived with our eerie sense of exposure to the world on the pages of our hometown newspaper and in the nightly TV newscast. We couldn't resist. We had to keep turning on the news, opening the *Denver Post*.

The Carefree Guest Home was a multi-winged three-story complex of red brick that housed 85 residents—a "rathole," according to one longtime Denver social worker who knew the place. Nearly a week after Mike's death, when *Post* reporter Pat McGuire visited Mike's room, the bed lay unmade, "stained with the death throes of the previous weekend. The remnants of the dead man's last cigarettes still filled an ashtray on the floor next to his bed. A worn paperback Western novel lay on his dresser." The room had "no carpets and worn furnishings. Newspapers were stacked in a corner, the dresser was cluttered with personal effects and a window stood open, allowing a cold breeze to air the room."

Mike evidently died during a seizure. Though his autopsy "failed to reveal an anatomical cause of death," the coroner concluded that his death resulted from "some type of seizure disorder."

From headline to last line, the *Denver Post* articles swooped in to rake Mom's emotions raw with every word. The local television stations took cameras into Mike's room. I watched the images with dread. Dark wood, cigarette butts, harsh light, loneliness incarnate—what Kierkegaard calls "quiet lostness... So many live... away from themselves and vanish like shadows. Their immortal souls are blown away...they are already disintegrated before they die."

The press used Mike's death as the hook in their exposé of poorly managed and tawdry guest homes. I felt vulnerable and accused, though the journalists made no mention of Mike's family and never showed up on our doorstep.

I don't remember how long Mom paced. That first indelible heart-clutching image of her overwhelms any details from succeeding days, searing a defining image of immeasurable sorrow in my memory.

After a week, I returned to Tucson. My letter home in mid-January ends with, "Hope things have settled down to normal. Or at least are settling. Keep listening to Dad's harangues, Mom. They're all true."

Of course things hadn't "settled down to normal." But I was back in my own life, far from our house in Denver, and I was eager to have my certainties about my steadfast parents return and click into reassuring place.

Isabelle and Don had Mike cremated. They chose to have no memorial service. Charlotte, predictably, didn't understand. She never forgave my mother for her choices in Mike's life and death. Char told me, "Your mother wouldn't bury him. And I didn't like that. Your mother didn't want any part of him, even after death. He was her son. She bore him, and it seems to me she could have buried him. She didn't want anybody to know he belonged to her."

Charlotte had it wrong. Our mother knew she was incapable of the emotional fortitude that Mike's funeral or memorial gathering would require. My parents grieved, but they despised funerals, especially impersonal religious ones. They had no concerns about the Jewish taboo on cremation. They prepaid for their own cremations decades before they died.

Our parents had the crematory disperse Mike's ashes. After my own intimate experiences with Isabelle's and Don's ashes, and my nostalgic list of places to scatter them, I admit to being troubled by that final lack of ceremony, by Mike completely and utterly vanishing. Handling our parents' ashes helped me grieve. I'm not convinced our parents' choices for Mike—no memorial, no grave, no family gathering to spread his remains—helped with their mourning.

With those framed photos of Mike she had always kept on her bedroom dresser, Mom granted Mike a place to look back at her every day. Now she took down the pictures and moved into storage this tangible declaration of love and connection, archiving the photos in a box labeled "family history." Maybe their removal signified her realization that the constancy of courage required to confront Mike's tragedy was no longer necessary. An acknowledgment of Mike's absence, of her loss, of closure. Or maybe she no longer had sufficient resolve, the daily determination to grapple with Mike's gaze.

Mike died. And he disappeared.

But not quite yet. Not until the press finished with his story.

CHAPTER SEVEN

*This could cause a great deal of publicity for me
which I think they should know about someday. The public.*
—Mike's letter to Isabelle, June 10, 1967

RICHARD CLARK, who ran the Carefree
Guest Home, told *Denver Post* reporter Pat
McGuire that "Mike was certainly disabled with
epilepsy." Disability might have come from his
medication—or over-medication. No mention
of mental illness or intellectual challenges. Mike
was "often given to seizures, though able to get
around by himself, go to the doctor by himself
and leave the home to visit friends."

Friends? I'm glad he had them. But who were
they? Can I rely on Clark's report? It's easier for
me to define Mike as a mentally ill tragedy than
as a guy with a life, with friends, with Wild West
books on his nightstand.

With Mike's public death transformed into
a story about Denver's shoddy boarding houses,

Pat McGuire had a reason to ask about the backstory of this young man who had died. In his newspaper pieces, the *Post* reporter constructs a snapshot of Mike at 33.

McGuire quotes Richard Clark, who describes Mike's days. "We had a lot of sympathy for him. He was sick. He just moved slow. He never did feel good. He was sort of the worrying type...every time he had an ache he would worry."

These few words contain the epitaph for Mike's personhood, the full content of his personality profile. I've encountered no more detail anywhere.

I picture Mike dragging through his years, one day very much like the next. I've visited today's versions of board-and-care homes, and there are always a few folks waiting in the dark lobbies, needing help from the staff to address glitches in their prescriptions or paperwork. This is their occupation—managing the details of their relationship with multiple layers of confusing bureaucracy.

I also wonder if Mike's "worrying" was Clark's shorthand for Mike's long-ago diagnosis of

paranoia. Many people living with schizophrenia hear voices that worry them and live with
debilitating concerns about conspiracies. Mike's
worries might have been mundane, or they might
have been crippling.

Clark called "the Mike Trimble problem"
a "slipup." The staff member who should have
checked on Mike over the weekend "was snowed
under." But as the *Post* pursued this story, Patrick
McGuire discovered that two other residents of
the ironically-named Carefree Guest Home had
also died unnoticed in recent months. Clark
pleaded good intentions and rationalized, re-
minding readers he lacked sufficient funding to
run a fully competent operation.

In the days following Mike's death, the director of the Colorado Commission on the Disabled
demanded a hearing to investigate Carefree. "I'm
not thinking so much of those three who have
already died, " he said, "but of the other 85 residents there. How many of them were not seen
over the weekend but did not die? I'm concerned
about these people." Despite Richard Clark's

When Mike lived here, this was the Carefree Guest Home. Today it's Fairview Place Lofts. The building is just 2 1/2 miles from our family home, where Mike spent half his childhood.

complaints about being "woefully underfunded" and notwithstanding his comment to Pat McGuire that staffers frequently "stay up all night helping someone through an emotional problem," I'm with the disability commission director. How could Clark and his underpaid staff properly attend to 85 needy people?

Denver city health officials and the city attorney's office were especially interested in "whether Trimble's apparent seizure, if it had been noticed, could have been treated and his death prevented." The city coroner's office couldn't determine from Mike's autopsy "whether death occurs during or subsequent" to a seizure. The Division of Public Health began an "in-depth investigation" and promised to turn over their results to the city attorney's office for possible further action.

By the 21st of January, the city attorney concluded that Richard Clark "appeared to have violated city regulations governing personal-care boarding homes," which require checking on residents at least daily. But the city health officials issued only "a severe reprimand" to Clark and his Carefree Guest Home. Dr. Paul Kuhn, director of Denver's Personal Health Service, said of Clark, "He has made some significant improvements."

Pat McGuire enumerated these changes in the *Post*, a list that seemed to begin and end with "...a procedure each morning at breakfast, where staffers write down the names of those eating. Anyone not in the breakfast line is sought out and checked."

"That's a real step forward," Kuhn, the health official, told McGuire, though this new rule sounds like a small effort, indeed. The city gave Clark a break because of poor funding that left the guest home perpetually understaffed. "My knowledge of this situation tempers what I have recommended," Kuhn said. "This is more than a Denver problem. It's a statewide problem. It's a great societal problem."

True enough. Meanwhile, the authorities backed off. Three people dead, perhaps unnecessarily. Reprimand issued. Case closed.

CHOOSING EMPATHY

My mother never thought of herself as strong, but she was. Isabelle beat the odds bestowed by her inheritance of an inordinate number of family sorrows. Bipolar disorder, schizophrenia, abuse. Disability, depression, rejection, and lies. Alcoholism, abandonment, suicide, and madness scattered misfortune through her family and her life.

I'm grateful to mostly have avoided these calamities, the hazards that run in our genes. I'm grateful my children have, as well.

I didn't escape unscathed. I've opened The Mike File. I've held the letters and the stories and the grief in my hands. I've felt tender, I've felt vulnerable. I've felt fear about what I'd find. And I've realized that I define myself, in part, as Not-Mike. I've supposed I was a simple, stable person by nature, and maybe that's true. But when I saw how hard Mike was on our family, I surely chose to be the opposite.

I've ventured back into the past as the man I am now, content, in my sixties. I began with research, my comfort food. I tracked down documents—Isabelle's and Morey's divorce records, Morey's death certificate, Mike's autopsy report. I untangled family history, interviewed psychiatrists and social workers and elders in the Denver and Butte Jewish communities. I tracked the evolution of mental health treatment in 20th Century America. I asked obscure cousins and my difficult Aunt Charlotte to share their unvarnished memories. I met Morey Sher's surviving family.

I reconstructed Morey's life, finally discovering how he found his way to the family store in Livingston, Montana—where he met Mom's mother, who set him up with Isabelle. Morey had worked as a clerk in nearby Yellowstone National Park. What an ironic twist for Mike, who always dismissed my father's connection to nature and the outdoors as boring and meaningless.

As I reconstructed Isabelle's life and heritage, as I traced the parallel tracks of Mike's journey and the history of our treatment of mental illness, all these notes and words and drafts eventually brought me back to myself.

Mike's life brings me closer to my own life. Closer than I've ever been to knowing myself.

I also realize that I never separated fully from my parents. My wife, Joanne, reading draft after draft of this book, urged me to replace all those

Steve, wearing his cowboy duds at 4 1/2,
Mike at 12; Denver, 1955.

"we"s with "I." She kept telling me, with exasperation, "This book is not about 'we.' It's about *you*!"

And I kept answering, "But that's how my parents and I *felt*! It's a family story." But I finally got it when Joanne said, "Your parents could have written this. You weren't Mike's parent, you were his brother! How did *you* feel?"

I'm shocked that self-realization takes so long. But now I no longer think of myself as "mostly an only child." Mike was there, too, all along, shaping our family, shaping me. And his disappearance from our family was a grievous loss. I was deprived of a relationship with my brother, and that was a subtraction from what would have been a richer life for both of us.

I've come in from the garage where, it turns out, I've been hiding for more than sixty years. I've rejoined my family, even if many of them are gone. I've waited until I felt safe before I could own the mental illness that flares in our lineage through multiple generations. Finally, I can risk turning to each of these characters in my life with more understanding than I've ever before brought or sought.

Isabelle was a survivor. Immediately following Mike's death, she had to deal with my misguided two-year practice marriage, when I shifted my full emotional attention to a woman who rejected my mother. Mom had lost one son. Now, it looked to her like she was going to lose the remaining son, the "good" son. Isabelle crumpled. She spiraled into depression, but she came back out the other side, helped by therapy and by my father's loyalty, love—and protectiveness.

Don deferred to her vulnerability, to a fault. My father never saw stepping aside in social situations as anything other than an act of love. Only after Isabelle's death at 80 did he feel free to be completely himself. Only then did my wife, Joanne, truly come to know him.

As for me, a few more years of learning from relationships led to my marriage to Joanne in 1987—an equal partnership, a lifelong sense of family, a spouse who treated my parents with the same love and caring she gives to me.

As these people from my life drift away into memory, I don't want to lose them. My fragile raconteur of a mother. My kind, fierce scientist father. My stormcloud of a brother.

Generation to generation, we tumble along in a maze of family emotion and energy. The network of trails connecting these characters expands as elders die and new rounds of children appear and grow up in all of their challenging and endearing humanity.

In her essay, "The Empathy Exams," Leslie Jamison concludes that empathy "is a choice we make: to pay attention, to extend ourselves."

I arrived late, but I've made my choice.

THE BIG LEAP

We read editorials about The System's failures after mass shootings by loners, some with untreated mental illness. We read about police officers murdering the mentally ill, heartbreakingly repetitive scenarios where officers start shooting when social workers should have been talking. Meanwhile, our sons and daughters and friends struggle valiantly—and with no hint of violence directed outward—each coping without effective therapy and in inappropriate settings with the daily terror of bipolar disorder, psychosis, and depression. We know a lot about what can help, but mental illness has a weak lobby when legislatures vote on budgets.

If we could do our best for people with schizophrenia, just what is that best practice? What could Mike's life have been if we had done right by him when he returned to Denver in 1966? Surely, in this different world, Mike may not have been as disabled—and dismissed and sidelined—by his condition.

At the end of *American Psychosis*, writer and psychiatrist E. Fuller Torrey ventures to summarize what we've learned and what we should do for our fellow citizens who live with serious mental illnesses. Though mainstream psychiatry reveres Torrey, I know he's controversial. Robert Whitaker, another writer whose books have guided me, exchanges fiery Internet posts with Torrey. Whitaker aligns with the "consumers" and "survivors" who campaign against forced treatment while Torrey believes that people with the most severe mental illness should be required by law to be medicated.

So I'll listen to both Whitaker and Torrey as I imagine the best possible care for Mike, who would now be in his 70s. Instead of his actual trajectory—returning to Denver at 23 and dying in a "rathole" at 33—I'll build an alternate universe. I'll paint a picture that's better than what America has ever been able to offer in the underfunded disappointment of the real world. My ideal, though, is not unreachable.

With forethought, with leadership, with efficient distribution of the millions of dollars we now waste, this could have been Mike's life. This still could be the life of millions of other people like Mike.

Mike tries living alone, but he finds solo apartments isolating. He prefers the group home run by the non-profit Coalition for the Homeless where he lives with eight other men and women he's known for years. Mike has lived in the same northwest Denver cottage for more than two decades. The staff know him and like him. Group meetings in the house keep the members of the little community in touch with each other. As each resident negotiates the Denver treatment world, staff members can stay aware of changing needs and brainstorm solutions to accommodate these ups and downs.

Mike's seizures require medication. He also takes a low dose of a newer anti-psychotic drug. He and his doctors have figured out the minimum dosage to keep him above the threshold of disabling psychosis and depression without serious side-effects or complete loss of his self.

He held minimum wage jobs over the years, but he's now let these go. Money to pay for Mike's needs comes from Medicaid and SSI through the state to the city of Denver, which manages all mental health services and takes full responsibility for the care of people who live with a mental disorder.

Mike's team from the Mental Health Center of Denver includes a psychiatrist, a psychologist, a psychiatric nurse, a social worker, a peer from another group home, a case manager to help Mike negotiate the bureaucracy, a community council volunteer from the neighborhood. These folks check in with Mike frequently, and he can reach any of them via a hotline. Together with Mike, they make decisions about his care. The city of Denver and the state of Colorado conduct frequent unannounced inspections of Mike's home to keep the staff attentive.

Mike joins regular group therapy sessions. When his psychosis flares, there is always a crisis-respite bed for him in a facility that feels more like home than hospital. He returns to his own home as soon as he regains stability. He has come to terms with a difficult imperative; he takes his meds.

Mike has another community down the street, a drop-in consumer-run "clubhouse." Mike works here, as he has for years, taking his shift answering phones, neatening up. He loves the musical gatherings, and he's in charge of keeping the aging CD collection organized and safe. He still prefers the rock and roll of his youth.

And, now, the big leap.

After Mike broke off relations with our family, his team interceded. When our parents and I returned from the field season in Idaho in the fall of 1967, Mike's psychologist and social worker began to work out family visits that minimized conflict. We met on neutral ground. Sometimes, Isabelle saw Mike without my father or me. The connection wasn't always easy, but we maintained contact, seeing him when he was at his best. We moved past our awkwardness, and Mike's resentment softened.

The caregivers provided Isabelle with support, as well. A group of families who also had children with a mental illness met regularly to swap ideas and kindnesses. Our mother became a pioneering member of the National Alliance on Mental Illness. She served for years on the Jefferson County board of NAMI.

Mike maintained contact with Morey Sher's family, as well. Though his biological father had no interest in Mike, Morey had passed his son along to the other Shers, who valued the relationship, wrote letters, telephoned. Whenever Mike's Sher cousins came to town, they arranged a get-together.

With so much support, Mike stayed in touch. He called every week or two to speak with our mother.

He treated Don with less anger. He stayed interested in my life. And I visited him when I came to Denver.

These visits were short, but Mike knew I was out there. He knew my wife. He met our kids. He came to Isabelle's memorial service. He even came to Don's.

And, now, I am his surviving family. I am Mike's brother. I return to Denver every few months to see him. We go to concerts when there's an oldie group in town that he wants to see. I communicate with his treatment team. We're connected.

Mike turned 78 on New Year's Eve. I drove to Denver in January to visit him.

I pull in and park in front of his home. He's expecting me. I open the door to see my white-haired and grizzled brother slouched on the couch, watching television, smoking a cigarette, chatting with his friends. He turns toward me. He smiles.

"Hello, Steve. It's good to see you."

"Happy birthday, brother," I say. "I'm glad to see you, too."

END NOTES

Chapter One

Page 7: Psychiatrist John Edwards told Ron Powers, "I think primal fear is the origin, regarding mental illness, of all the misinformation, the projections, the denial, the blaming of the victim or the patient, the lack of empathy toward the sufferers, treating adolescents as criminals, cutting budgets for treatment centers—all of it. Human beings are terrified of this disease, and they try to deny it out of existence."

Ron Powers, *No One Cares About Crazy People: the chaos and heartbreak of mental health in America*, Hachette Books, New York & Boston, 2017. Page 5.

My book joins a robust genre of books by writers who have dealt with family members with mental illness. They (we) weave together personal stories with the history of treatment. Ron Powers' book is a stellar example. See also Pete

Earley, *Crazy: A Father's Search Through America's Mental Health Madness*, G.P. Putnam's Sons, New York, 2006.

Chapter Two

Page 22: History of special-ed programs in Jefferson County: http://www.arcjc.org/articles/winter2011/history.html (accessed on 12 May 2012).

Page 24: Louise L. Hay, *You Can Heal Your Life*, Hay House, 1999. "Illness in our body," page 9; bad eyes, page 153.

Chapter Three

Page 45: Zimmerman quote from interview with Margie O'Leary, retired psych tech and nurse, Colorado State Hospital, Pueblo, Colorado, July 8, 2013.

Page 46: Colorado State Hospital history from *The 13th Street Review: A Pictorial History of the Colorado State Hospital (Now CMHIP)* by Nell Mitchell. CMHIP Museum, Pueblo, Colorado, 2009.

Page 47-49: Robert Whitaker briskly guides us through the history of mental illness and treatment in the United States in *Mad in America: Bad Science, Bad Medicine, and the Enduring Mistreatment of the Mentally Ill* (Perseus, 2002). Californians on sterilization, p. 62. "America's concentration camps," P. 66. "chemical lobotomy," P. 144.

Page 47: 1963 figure on 500 people living in U.S. mental institutions involuntarily sterilized: *Out of Bedlam: the Truth about Deinstitutionalization*, Ann Braden Johnson, Basic Books, 1990.

Page 48: Montana State Hospital details: "The Right to Procreate: The Montana State Board of Eugenics and Body Politics" http://montanawomenshistory.org/the-right-to-procreate-the-montana-state-board-of-eugenics-and-body-politics/ (accessed 11 June 2014)

Page 53: Colorado Governor Steve McNichols quotes: "State Hospital's Ugly Past Recalled," Dennis Darrow, *The Pueblo Chieftain*, March 3, 1992.

Page 54: The Colorado State Hospital and Related Services for the Mentally Ill in Colorado,

U.S.: A Survey Report." *National Institute of Mental Health, National Institutes of Health, Public Health Service, Department of Health Education and Welfare.* 1958. Typescript in Colorado Mental Health Institute Museum archives, 23 pp.

Page 54: In my 75-cent Signet paperback edition (1960) of Dariel Telfer's *The Caretakers,* Simon & Schuster, 1959, Kathy's description of the male ward appears on pp. 154-157. The *New York Times* review appears here: https://www.nytimes.com/1959/11/22/archives/life-in-a-snakepit-the-caretakers-by-dariel-telfer-404-pp-new-york.html (accessed 9 July 2020)

The novel, now nearly forgotten, has a great backstory, as recounted by legendary editor Michael Korda in *Another Life: A Memoir of Other People* (Delta, New York, 2000). Telfer found an agent by accident, a charlatan who claimed to be a French count and who had briefly represented Somerset Maugham. Korda acquired the book for Simon & Schuster at the beginning of his career, and with his boss, another legendary editor, Bob Gottlieb, toned down the sex and tightened the story with major rewriting. Telfer, a "plump, gentle woman" remained "graceful and kind" when her book set a record for pre-publication paperback rights—and launched Korda's career.

Page 59: JFK speech: "reliance on the cold mercy of custodial isolation" to "the open warmth of community concern and capability." From: http://www.jfklibrary.org/Asset-Viewer/Archives/JFKPOF-052-012.aspx (accessed 9 May 2013)

Page 68: "Treatment of Chronic Schizophrenic Reactions with Reserpine," Leo E. Hollister, George E. Krieger, Alan Kringel, Richard H. Roberts, *Annals of the New York Academy of Sciences* Volume 61, Reserpine in the Treatment of Neuropsychiatric, Neurological, and Related Clinical Problems pages 92–100, April 1955. [statistics on prevalence of schizophrenia diagnosis] http://onlinelibrary.wiley.com/doi/10.1111/nyas.1955.61.issue-1/issuetoc (accessed 4 February 2016)

Page 68: Schizophrenia as "a wastebasket diagnostic classification:" *A Critical History of Schizophrenia*, Kieran McNally, Basingstoke, UK: Palgrave Macmillan 2016. PP. 153-154.

Page 69: Genetic components of schizophrenia: *The Gene: An Intimate History*, Siddhartha Mukherjee, Scribner, 2016. page 300.

Page 69: "Nearly half of people with one mental disorder meet the diagnostic criteria for two or more disorders." NIH press release, June 6, 2005: "Mental Illness Exacts Heavy Toll, Beginning in Youth." http://www.nimh.nih.gov/news/science-news/2005/mental-illness-exacts-heavy-toll-beginning-in-youth.shtml (accessed 6 July 2015)

Page 70: Grand jury findings: "Pueblo Grand Jury Blasts State Hospital Program," *Colorado Springs Gazette-Telegraph*, May 19, 1962. "Commingling of Male and Female Patients Denounced by Grand Jury." *The Pueblo Chieftain*, May 18, 1962.

Chapter Four

Page 82: Leslie Jamison, *The Empathy Exams*, Graywolf Press, Minneapolis, 2014. page 7: on entering another person's pain.

Page 83: Brené Brown on shame, TED Talk, March 2012. http://www.ted.com/talks/

brene_brown_listening_to_shame.html   (accessed 15 May 2013)

Page 84: Brené Brown on connection: *Daring Greatly: How the Courage to Be Vulnerable Transforms the Way We Live, Love, Parent, and Lead*. Gotham Books, 2012. page 68.

Page 91: Blame the "schizophrenogenic" mother: Andrew Solomon: *Far From the Tree: Parents, Children, and the Search for Identity*, Scribner, 2012. P. 307.

Chapter Five

Page 104: Info on chronic mentally ill not returning to families: *Out of Bedlam: the Truth about Deinstitutionalization*, Ann Braden Johnson, Basic Books, 1990. P. 74.

Page 104: In *Hidden Valley Road: Inside the Mind of an American Family* (Doubleday, 2020), Robert Kolker narrates the astonishing story of the Galvin family in Colorado Springs.

Page 105: Number of State Hospital releases in Denver boarding homes, from: Colorado State Hospital Memorandum; Denver Area

Coordinator's Office Annual Report, June 19, 1970, by Claire Stahley. Colorado State Hospital Museum archives.

Page 110: my subhead comes from two quotes. Writer and therapist Ann Braden Johnson notes that the majority of folks released from state hospitals go to group homes (also called board-and-care homes), "the modern version of the almshouse." *Out of Bedlam: the Truth about Deinstitutionalization*, Ann Braden Johnson, Basic Books, 1990. p. 124.

And pediatrician and writer Mark Vonnegut writes of the bravery of the mentally ill from the perspective of someone who has lived through psychotic breaks himself. "If we're lucky enough to get better, we have to deal with people who seem unaware of our heroism and who treat us as if we are just mentally ill." Mark Vonnegut, *Just Like Someone Without Mental Illness Only More So*, Delacorte Press, 2010. p. 5.

Page 112: Robert Whitaker, *Mad in America: Bad Science, Bad Medicine, and the Enduring Mistreatment of the Mentally Ill*, Perseus, 2002. "friendless existences," p. 190.

Chapter Six

Page 118: *Denver Post* stories about Mike:
—"Death Knocked…but Only Mike Was Listening." Patrick A. McGuire, 12/16/1976.
—"Guest Home Gets Denver Probe."12/20/1976
Patrick A. McGuire
—"Case of Missing Patient: He's 'Dying of Loneliness.'" Patrick A. McGuire (12/21/1976)
—"Guest Home to Get 'Severe Reprimand.'" Patrick A. McGuire, 1/21/1977

Chapter Seven

Page 133: Statistics on heritability of bipolar disorder: http://schizophrenia.com/moodswing%20pages/genetics.html (accessed 12 January 2016).

Page 138: Leslie Jamison, *The Empathy Exams*, Graywolf Press, Minneapolis, 2014: empathy "is a choice we make: to pay attention, to extend ourselves." p. 23.

Page 139: E. Fuller Torrey, *American Psychosis: How the Federal Government Destroyed the Mental Illness Treatment System*, Oxford University Press, 2014. Robert Whitaker, *Mad in America: Bad Science, Bad Medicine, and the Enduring Mistreatment of the Mentally Ill*, Perseus, 2002. Robert Whitaker, *Anatomy of an Epidemic: Magic Bullets, Psychiatric Drugs, and the Astonishing Rise of Mental Illness in America*, Crown, 2010.

ACKNOWLEDGMENTS

First, I thank my mother and father, Isabelle and Don Trimble, for everything. For their love, for their strength, and for their archivist inclinations that led to saving all these letters, documents, and photographs.

I couldn't have written this book without the openness of the many people I interviewed, who generously shared memories, expertise, family records and photographs. Much of my research supports this book between the lines and behind the scenes. The final text may leave out their direct quotes, but I never could have reached this point without the help of the people I acknowledge here.

In my family, I thank: Sarah Bee, Denise Brinig, Jackie Cooper, Merry Elkins, Teri Faychild, Patty Hawley, Joan Hirschfeld, John Gerecht, Gary Goodman, Judith Lauterstein, Lisa O'Loughlin, Linda Rubin Royer, Cathy Rubin, Leslie Sweetbaum, and Debbie and Dave

Wasserman. In Morey Sher's family: Hank Hoffman, Molly Hoffman, Andi Penner, Len Sher, Bernie Vallens, and Nita Vallens. Crucial stories came from the late Myron Brinig, Hannah Sher Rivkin Licht, and Charlotte Rubin.

In Butte: the helpful staff at the Butte-Silver Bow Archives and Lew Rudolph.

In Pueblo: Ann Courtright, Brett Cozza and Michael Mihalas of Friendly Harbor, Tene` Greenhood, Mary Mehess, Nell and Bob Mitchell at the Colorado Mental Health Institute Museum, and Margie O'Leary.

In Denver (and those who lived in Denver but later dispersed widely): Jeanne Abrams, Theresa Baiotto, David Burgess at CHARG, Joe Cahn at the Jewish Genealogical Society of Colorado, Richard Cohn, Anne Enderby, Robert Freedman, Jean Greenberg, Wally Hansen, Moe Keller, Don Krill, Susan Manning, Kathleen Mullen, Anne Richtel, Libby and Marc Rosen, Marijo Rymer, Youlon Savage, Glenda Slade, Sherry Stark, Rebecca Watt, Thyria Wilson, and Zelda Witkind.

Friends and family read the manuscript as I created it, and their input was invaluable: Steve and Lois Baar, Peggy Battin, Harriet Choice, Dana Cope, Jennifer Dewey, Neysa Dickey, David Gessner, Mary Gibson, Denise Goldsmith, Sue Gorey, Martha Ham, Peggy Hansen, Gail Hochman, Amy Kaplan, Janet Kaufman, Gary Nabhan, Roz Newmark, Andi Penner, Ray and Catherine Petros, Jill Poyer, Joe Riddle, Bill Slotnik, Joanne Slotnik, Judy Smith, Theresa Wilson, and Annie and Mark Zarn. Angela Kimball at NAMI helped me imagine the best care for Mike in a kinder world.

As always, my writing group in Salt Lake City provided crucial guidance and support: Melissa Bond, Brenda Sue Cowley, Gretchen Hummel, Dave Jones, Kevin Jones, Dorothee Kocks, David Kranes, Kurt Proctor, and Amie Tullius. My book group read my first full draft, applying critical reading skills honed by 28 years of monthly meetings: Howard Bartlett, Nick Carling, Andrew Dodds, Doug Goldsmith, Kevin Havlik, Rob Mayer, Chuck Smith, and Mark Vlasic.

In Salt Lake City, Anne Pendo assisted with tracking down medical records. Melanie Battistone helped interpret Mike's school tests. Cheryl Palmer generously talked me through Mike's autopsy report. My friends Jack and Joyce Dolcourt and Nick Carling provided introductions to their family connections in Denver's Jewish community. And I had a lively discussion of an early draft with an Osher Lifelong Learning class at the University of Utah thanks to Tika Beard.

In January 2019, I had the opportunity to tell Mike's story on stage at The Bee, Salt Lake City's venue for community storytelling, inspired by NPR's The Moth. This experience brought me closer to the emotional core of my experience with my brother than ever before. I've tried to bring that connection back to this book. Many thanks to The Bee's Giuliana Serena and Nan Seymour for skillful mentoring.

Leslie Browning has created a warm community as well as a vital small press at Homebound Publications. Many thanks to her for shepherding my book with care and professionalism through every step of the publishing process.

Lastly, my wife and kids live inside my books with me as I work my way through each project. My wife, Joanne, is my fiercest critic; I love her, and I love her editing. Dory and Jake found much in this story new to them, and I am pleased to connect our children with so much of their heretofore unknown past.

Mike, life dealt you such a raw deal. I knew you when I was six, and then again when I was 16. And then I let you slip away for more than fifty years. This was my loss.

I'm glad I know you—at least a little—now.

Salt Lake City, 2021

ABOUT THE AUTHOR

Stephen Trimble tells stories—in words and photographs—about the land and people of the West. *The Mike File* is his 25ᵗʰ book—as writer, photographer, or editor.

The breadth of his awards mirrors the wide embrace of his work: The Sierra Club's Ansel Adams Award for photography and conservation; The National Cowboy Museum's Western Heritage "Wrangler" Award; and an honorary Doctor of Humane Letters from his alma mater, Colorado College. Artists of Utah chose Trimble as one of Utah's "15 Most Influential Artists" in 2019.

He speaks and writes frequently as a conservation advocate and has taught writing at the University of Utah, where he received a Wallace Stegner Fellowship at the Tanner Humanities Center during the centennial of Stegner's birth. Trimble lives in Salt Lake City and Torrey, Utah, where his family proudly stewards a Nature Conservancy conservation easement in the redrock canyons of the Colorado Plateau—a story he tells in *Bargaining for Eden: The Fight for the Last Open Spaces in America*. For more about his work, see www.stephentrimble.net.

HOMEBOUND
PUBLICATIONS

We are an award-winning independent publisher founded in 2011 striving to ensure that the mainstream is not the only stream. More than a company, we are a community of writers and readers exploring the larger questions we face as a global village. It is our intention to preserve contemplative storytelling. We publish full-length introspective works of creative non-fiction, literary fiction, and poetry. *Fly with us into our 10th year.*

WWW.HOMEBOUNDPUBLICATIONS.COM

LITTLE
BOUND BOOKS

THE LITTLE BOUND BOOKS ESSAY SERIES

———

WWW.LITTLEBOUNDBOOKS.COM

LOOK FOR OUR TITLES WHEREVER BOOKS ARE SOLD

Printed in the USA
CPSIA information can be obtained
at www.ICGtesting.com
JSHW022345140824
68134JS00019B/1695

9 781953 340221